Waldorf School Method of Painting

Waldorf School Method of Painting

Kytka Hilmar-Jezek

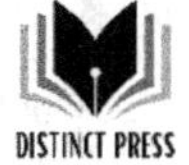

Distinct Press Publishing.
www.distinctpress.com | US+ 727-238-7884

Library of Congress Cataloging-in-Publication Data

Hilmar-Jezek, Kytka 1964-
Waldorf School Method of Painting / Kytka Hilmar-Jezek

Summary: Guided by the principles of anthroposophy and Waldorf education, *Waldorf School Method of Painting* explores the profound significance of color in the lives of children, fostering self-expression, imagination, and inner growth. With practical guidance, step-by-step instructions, and insights into the moral and ethical aspects of color, this book invites readers to embark on a journey of painting, from watercolors to plant pigments. Celebrating the seasons, capturing nature's moods, and emphasizing the importance of setting the mood, this book inspires educators, parents, and art enthusiasts to nurture the artistic spirit within and forge a deeper connection to the world of colors and beauty. – Provided by publisher.

ISBN- 978-1-943103-34-8

1. Education & Teaching > Schools & Teaching > Homeschooling 2. Education & Teaching > Schools & Teaching > Instruction Methods > Arts & Humanities 3. Education & Teaching > Schools & Teaching > Parent Participation 4. Waldorf School Method of Painting 5. Hilmar-Jezek, Kytka

"The task of art is to take hold of the shining, the radiance, the manifestation, of that which as spirit weaves and lives throughout the world. All genuine art seeks the spirit. Even when art wishes to represent the ugly, the disagreeable, it is concerned, not with the sensory - disagreeable as such, but with the spiritual which proclaims its nature in the midst of unpleasantness. If the spiritual shines through the ugly, even the ugly becomes beautiful. In art it is upon a relation to the spiritual that beauty depends."

- Rudolf Steiner

Contents

Acknowledgments

I offer my heartfelt gratitude to Rudolf Steiner, whose profound philosophy has served as a guiding light throughout my journey. It is through his wisdom that I have come to grasp the true essence of education and the pivotal role of a teacher. Steiner's teachings have enlightened me to the fundamental truth that a teacher, who can assume any form, holds the sacred responsibility of nurturing within the child a lifelong passion for learning. His invaluable insights have shaped my understanding, inspiring me to embark on the path of education with unwavering dedication and a deep-rooted commitment to fostering the innate curiosity and love for knowledge that resides within each young mind.

Above all, my deepest gratitude goes to my three beloved children, who have now blossomed into remarkable individuals at the ages of 30, 25, and 22. When I embarked on this profound journey, the availability of information was scarce, but what prevailed was an unwavering trust in my instincts and a profound commitment to allowing you to flourish at your own pace and pursue your own passions.

In those formative days, a flicker of doubt would occasionally creep into my thoughts, causing me to question if I was, in fact, toying with the very fabric of your lives. However, as I witness the extraordinary intelligence, boundless compassion, resounding success, and unwavering love that radiates from each one of you, I am overwhelmed with joy and gratitude that we embarked on this shared path of growth and discovery. Being both your mother and teacher has been an unparalleled privilege, and I wholeheartedly thank each and every one of you for unveiling the depths of my being and igniting the very best within me.

Zachary, Zanna, Zynnia; My love for you all transcends the limitations of words...

Preface

"The mind is not a vessel to be filled, but a fire to be kindled."
– Plutarch

Waldorf wet-on-wet watercolor painting is a technique commonly used in Waldorf education to engage children in the artistic process and stimulate their creativity. This approach involves painting on damp paper with watercolor paints, allowing the colors to blend and flow more freely.

The wet-on-wet technique is believed to offer a more immersive and sensory experience for children, as they can witness the colors merging and spreading on the paper. It encourages a sense of exploration and discovery, as children can observe how different hues interact with each other and how shapes and forms emerge from the fluidity of the colors.

One of the key aspects of Waldorf wet-on-wet watercolor painting is its focus on the process rather than the final outcome. This means that the emphasis is placed on the child's engagement, imagination, and personal expression rather than achieving a specific end result. The open-ended nature of the technique allows children to freely explore their creativity and develop their own unique artistic interpretations.

This painting technique is often introduced to children at a young age, as early as two or three years old, as it is considered accessible and developmentally appropriate for their abilities. It encourages fine motor skills development, hand-eye coordination, and an appreciation for color and texture.

In Waldorf education, wet-on-wet watercolor painting is often integrated into various subjects and activities, such as storytelling, nature exploration, and seasonal celebrations. It is seen as a means of fostering a deeper connection to the natural world and nurturing the child's sense of wonder and imagination.

“He who wants to experience the true being of color must not start from a preconceived idea of what to paint. He must wait and see what develops out of the colors themselves.”

Asked why an absolute amateur might want to draw or paint, many people might easily answer:

“To express one’s feelings.”

Expressing Oneself in Colors

When looking at painting through the lens of anthroposophy and Waldorf education, the approach to wet-on-wet watercolor painting takes on a therapeutic and transformative quality.

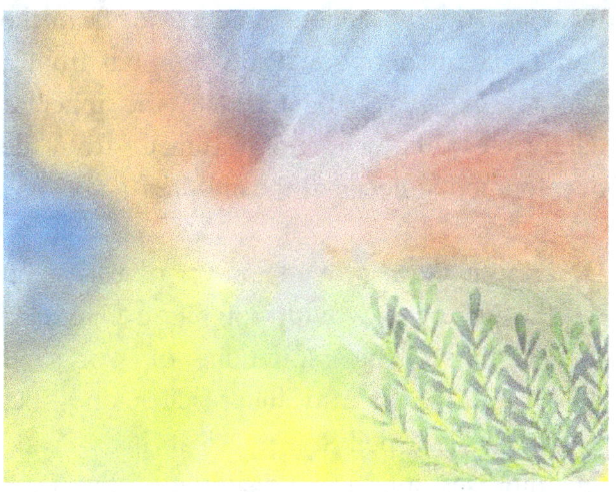

It is considered a profound experience to learn the art of utilizing the entire sheet of paper in a harmonious and efficient manner. This approach fosters a connection with color that goes beyond mere representation. Instead, it invites individuals to observe and surrender to the unfolding process, allowing the colors themselves to guide the brush rather than the dictates of one's personal emotions or preconceived ideas.

When encountering the paintings created by children in Waldorf schools or exhibitions, some may wonder why there is a certain similarity among them, why the children are not given complete freedom to paint as they wish. The answer lies in the understanding that these artistic expressions emerge not from the preferences of individual teachers, but from a path of exercises aligned with the inherent nature of color and attuned to the developmental needs of the children.

Describing the profound impact of early and intense experiences with color is a challenge that surpasses the limitations of words. It delves into the realm of inner riches, ones that cannot be grasped by physical hands, and encompasses qualities and subtleties that resist verbal description.

It is an undeniable truth that the world takes on a different hue for those who have embarked on a journey to comprehend the gentle, non-intellectual, yet deeply penetrating language of color. This awakening to the nuanced expressions of color bestows upon individuals a perspective that transcends the ordinary, infusing their lives with a heightened sensitivity to the profound beauty that permeates our existence.

The Role of Art

In the anthroposophical perspective and within the context of Waldorf education, engaging in artistic practices holds great significance. Through these practices, we encounter external challenges that present themselves in the form of materials to be worked with—colored paints, modeling clay, movement diagrams, or poetic works.

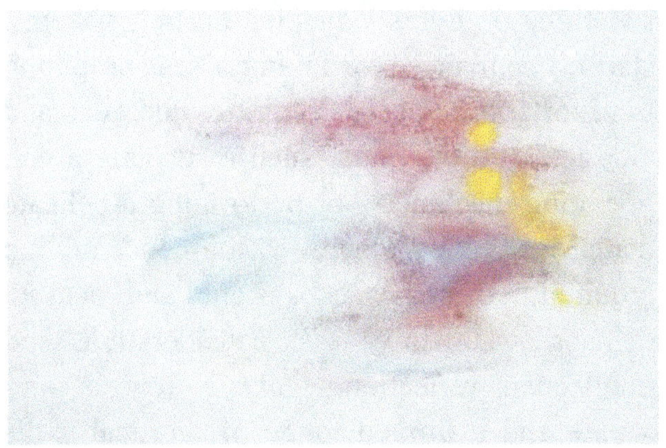

These challenges cannot be truly overcome unless we fully immerse ourselves in the materials, entering into a deep and intimate relationship with them. This process of entering into the material realm often evokes a wide range of feelings within our soul:

anticipation, disappointment, anger, resignation, contemplation, surprise, renewed hope, and the intense joy of creative expression. Yet, it is not solely within the realm of the soul that we feel this connection. It resonates deeply within our physical bodies, permeating our fingertips and toes.

The practice of an art holds particular significance in today's world. In an age dominated by technology, much of our daily actions are carried out automatically—switching on lights, adjusting heating systems, starting appliances, or taking a seat on public transportation. Some activities do demand alertness and attention, such as driving a car, operating machinery, or performing a delicate dental procedure. However, the concentration required in these instances is cool and focused, demanding attentiveness, consideration, and intellectual reflection. Only a few of our senses and a limited range of physical skills are called upon.

Engaging in an artistic activity places us in an entirely different situation. Here, routine alone cannot suffice. While full concentration is undoubtedly necessary, it encompasses a broad spectrum. Learning to drive a car may indeed be exciting, yet it cannot compare to the manifold and profound inner experiences that arise from modeling a form in clay, practicing a musical piece on an instrument, or embodying a character in a theatrical production.

In the world we inhabit today, there is a scarcity of physical activities that demand the wholehearted participation of body and soul. Artistic endeavors offer a precious opportunity to bridge this gap, providing a space where the physical and the spiritual intertwine, granting us access to profound depths of experience and a sense of unity with the world around us.

Children and Art

The profound connection between body and soul is a distinctive quality of childhood. Unlike adults who often strive to conceal their feelings and emotions, children naturally express themselves through their physical actions. When they are angry, they stomp their feet; when they are joyful, they jump up and down.

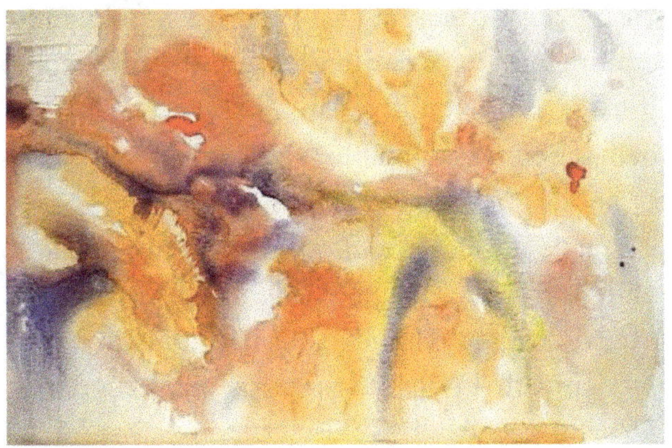

By providing children with opportunities to express their innermost feelings through artistic activities, we allow their deepest needs to find free expression. However, it is not a matter of merely giving them unrestricted freedom. Sometimes, the inner engagement of children in creative and artistic endeavors is mistakenly seen as a means for them to discharge pent-up emotions. If that were the case, we might as well let them pound on an empty tin can, run around aimlessly, or break china in the park.

But art is formative, both in the material realm and in the realm of the soul. Various artistic tasks may require a different inner attitude than the one we naturally adopt. In this way, a cautious child can be encouraged to be more daring, an exuberant child can learn to be more circumspect, a weak-willed child can develop greater perseverance, an obstinate child can become more adaptable, and so on.

The educational effects of artistic activities on children have been widely observed and acknowledged. However, it is not always fully recognized how far-reaching and enduring these effects can be.

The most deeply ingrained habits and behavioral patterns are formed during the imitation phase of a child's development. Some of these naturally change over the years in response to shifts in the environment and one's attitude towards life. However, others persist and remain hidden beneath the threshold of consciousness, resistant to change.

One such persistent pattern is the fundamental positive or negative attitude a child develops towards the environment and other people.

As educators (and homeschooling parents), we can strive to cultivate in children another profound instinct: the inclination to actively engage with everything they encounter in the outside world, to involve themselves in it, and to shape it. There is no other form of activity more suitable for nurturing this instinct, even in early childhood, than artistic activity.

Through artistic engagement, a child learns to wholeheartedly immerse themselves, with every fiber of their being, in the pursuit of solving a problem that is important not because it offers material gain but because it is inherently intriguing from a human perspective. Thus, a foundation is laid in the child for the capacity to genuinely take interest in the world around them later in life.

A Problem of Civilization

The notion of "taking an interest" may seem ordinary, but it carries profound significance when considering how we can best guide children and young people towards habits and pursuits that enrich and give purpose to their lives.

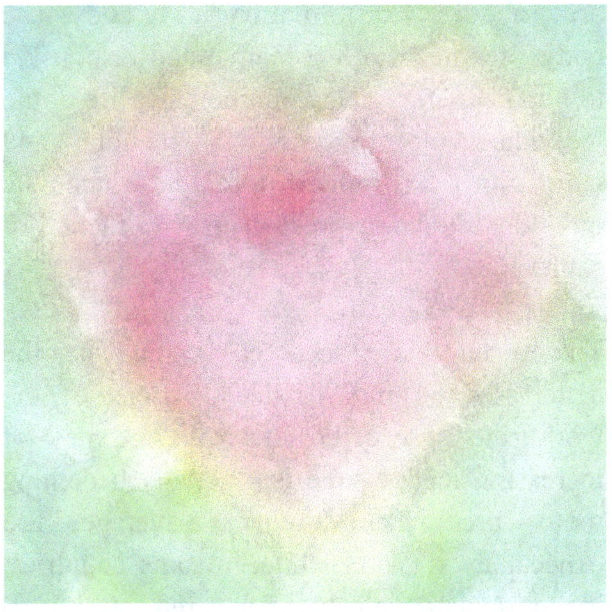

This is true especially for teenagers, who find themselves in a stage of life where everything appears uncertain, having a genuine interest to hold onto can be decisive for their entire future.

Why is it that an artistic inclination brings forth the capacity to generate and sustain vitality? Rudolf Steiner has shed light on this matter. He described how artistic activities, by opening up a wide range of soul experiences and fostering a close interplay between physical and psychic endeavors, gradually bring about a transformation in the body. The body becomes more receptive and responsive to impulses emerging from the inner life of the individual. It becomes a flexible and harmonious instrument through which the individuality can express itself with the aid of soul forces.

The earlier this process can commence, the better! In the industrialized nations of the world, the issue of how to make the most of increasing leisure time is gradually becoming more pressing. Moreover, average life expectancy is rising while, in some countries, the retirement age is being lowered.

People who possess a profound interest in global issues, as well as in the lives of those around them, and who thereby maintain liveliness and adaptability even in advanced years, tend to share certain common traits alongside their individual characteristics. They often possess an artistic disposition and a certain childlike openness. Such individuals can be found among the elderly in all walks of life. Some, like Leonardo da Vinci and Goethe, are celebrated in the annals of history, while others may be familiar to us as robust elderly friends or acquaintances.

It is not always the case that these individuals are professionally engaged in the arts, although even their manner of recounting events and incidents often carries an element of keen artistic sensibility, particularly if they hail from rural areas. Their robustness does not always arise from good physical health alone. Their vitality may simply reflect their capacity to be genuinely interested in the outside world or their ability to shield their ailments from those around them.

Children and Color

The ever-changing colors of the sky surround us in a mesmerizing display: radiant blues, almost black in the night, adorned with gray and white clouds, blending into mystical violets, ablaze with red, shining in yellow and orange, and delicate greens within the rainbow.

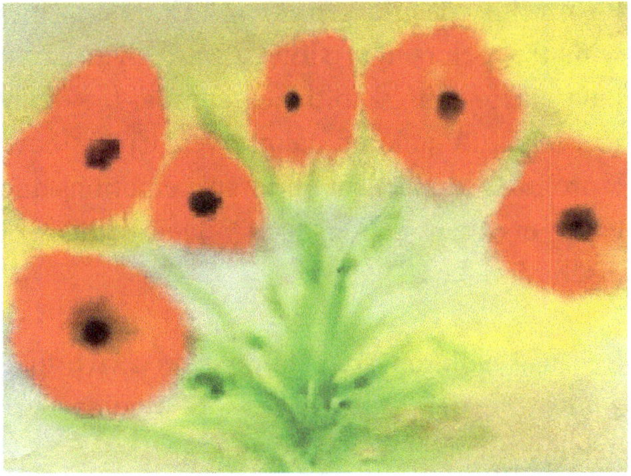

When we cast our gaze upon our surroundings, everything appears in color: the white snow, the gray stones, the blue-green sea, red apples, green meadows, yellow golden cornfields, violets, and brown cows.

From early childhood, we are immersed in the ever-changing colors of our environment. These colors influence our outlook on life, shape our moods, and find expression in the hues of our clothing. We take delight in adorning ourselves with chosen colors.

Children possess a natural affinity for colors. Even as infants, they reach out for colored objects that capture their attention. Soon, they begin to remember these colors and associate them with specific sensations. Children unite with the colors that flow toward them from their surroundings, to the extent that they may feel inwardly colored themselves. Colors have a profound impact on children's emotions and can evoke feelings of well-being or discomfort.

Because children are far more receptive than adults, their experiences of color are heightened and intensified.

During the early years, a child's sense perceptions are still fresh, and everything they perceive makes a lasting impression on their body. Consequently, it is not beneficial for a baby to be exposed too soon to harsh daylight or subjected to the lifeless glow of an electric lamp. The young child initially perceives light and color as varying degrees of brightness. Only through the interaction of light and color with their eyes does the organ of sight fully develop.

In his book "*The Education of the Child*," Rudolf Steiner elucidates the influence of color on a child: "A 'nervous,' that is, excitable child, should be treated differently in terms of their environment compared to a child who is calm and lethargic. Everything must be considered, from the color of the room and the objects commonly surrounding the child to the color of their clothing. An excitable child should be surrounded by and dressed in shades of red and reddish-yellow, while a lethargic child may benefit from the calming influence of blue or bluish-green tones. The crucial factor lies in the complementary color that arises within the child. In the case of red, it is green, and in the case of blue, it is orange-yellow."

Until they reach school age, many children may interchangeably identify red as green and green as red, and less frequently, blue as yellow and yellow as blue. Additionally, their favorite colors may change over time. For instance, a mother once shared with me that green had been her child's preferred color for a long time until she was nearly six, when she declared that red had taken its place.

This can be explained by the fact that initially, children experience the complementary color more intensely than the external color and only gradually come to perceive it as adults do.

The Moral Effect of Color

In our ordinary lives, we often perceive colors as attributes of the objects that surround us, rarely considering them as independent entities. However, to the inner vision of the soul, the essential nature of colors can be revealed.

This concept, known as the "sensory moral effect of color" or the "effect of color with reference to moral associations," was articulated by Johann Wolfgang von Goethe. Through excerpts from Goethe's "*Theory of Colors*", we can deepen our understanding of the nature of color.

The best way to introduce children to color is to let them paint with colors dissolved in water, for then the color in a liquid form will best reveal its nature.

The most effective way to introduce children to color is by allowing them to paint with watercolors. In this fluid form, colors can best reveal their true essence. Even children as young as two or three years old can handle a paintbrush and engage in the process of painting. They intuitively grasp the brush, dip it into the watercolor pot, and begin painting, gradually covering the entire white sheet of paper with colors. They may initially use only one color until the pot is empty, and then move on to another color, effortlessly layering it over the previous one. What matters most here is the activity of painting and the experience of creation. Yet, unbeknownst to them, the colors' effects are subtly unfolding within their bodies.

Children delight in painting with watercolors and become joyfully absorbed in the process. As they reach the age of three or four, they become more aware of the colors themselves. They begin to place one color next to another on the paper, carefully dipping their brushes into the pot, and becoming engrossed in the unfolding interplay of colors on the page.

Rudolf Steiner repetitively dictates that color must be inwardly shining, and that liquid paint should be used to create this in the right way.

In "*Colour*", by Rudolf Steiner p 49, Steiner says that a painting of a wall will not be a wall, only the image of one, unless the color is made luminous inwardly. He says:

"We must make the colors shine inwardly; they will then, in a certain sense, become mineralized. For this reason, it would be good to give up painting from the palette, which leads merely to smearing coloring matter onto a surface and makes it impossible to evoke the inwardly shining quality in the right way. We should try to paint increasingly from pots of liquid paint with colour that is liquid and has a flowing, shining quality. Generally speaking, the introduction of the palette has brought an

inartistic element into painting. The palette has brought a materialistic form of painting, a failure to understand the true nature of color - for color is never really absorbed by any material body but lives within it and emanates from it. Therefore, when I put my colors on to a surface I must make them shine inwardly".

Goethe's Wheel of Color

In the realm of colors, there exists a hue that is closest to the realm of light itself. It reveals its presence with even the slightest softening of illumination, whether it be through semi-transparent mediums or the gentle reflection from white surfaces.

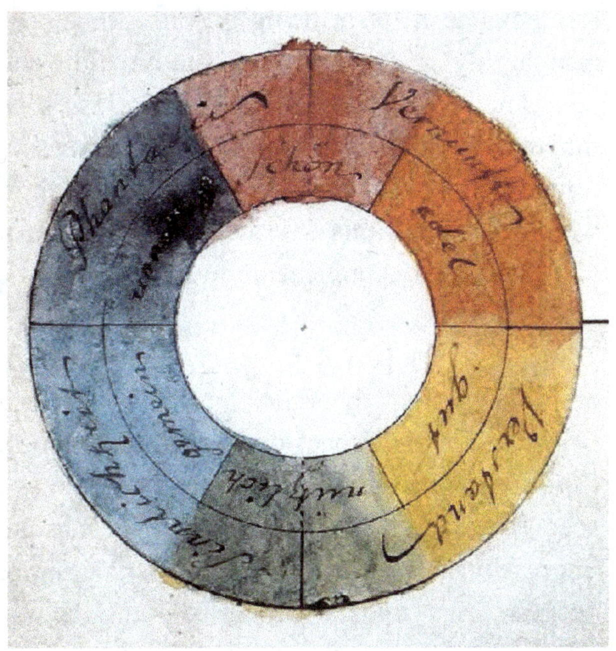

In experiments with prisms, this color expands and extends itself widely within the realm of light. It maintains its pure and exquisite form before mingling with blue to give rise to the green. This color, in its utmost purity, emanates warmth and beauty. Its effect can be vividly experienced when we observe a landscape through a yellow glass, especially on a gray winter's day. It brings delight to the eyes, expands and uplifts the heart, as if a radiant glow is directed towards us.

However, just as this color, in its pure and luminous state, is pleasing and uplifting, it is also highly susceptible to contamination and disharmony. If it becomes sullied or loses its inherent vitality, it can produce an unpleasant effect. For instance, the color of sulphur, which tends towards avarice, carries within it something that is unpleasing to behold.

The anthroposophical understanding of color emphasizes the dynamic interplay between colors and their impact on human experience. Colors possess qualities that can evoke specific moods, feelings, and spiritual impressions. By exploring these nuances, we deepen our understanding of the subtle relationship between color and the human soul. In the ever-evolving realm of colors, we find that no hue remains stagnant.

It is through a gentle condensing or darkening of yellow that we can easily witness its transformation into a reddish tone. As this process unfolds, the color gains in intensity, revealing itself in a powerful and resplendent red-yellow manifestation.

On the other hand, when we explore the combination of yellow and red, the active qualities of color reach their highest energy. It is not surprising that individuals who possess an impetuous and robust nature, often without extensive education, find particular pleasure in this color. Throughout the world, among savage nations, an inclination towards this hue has been universally observed. Even when children are left to their own devices in exploring colors, they rarely spare vermilion, drawn to its allure.

Blue, in its essence, carries with it a touch of darkness, contrasting the radiance that accompanies yellow. Just as the upper sky and distant mountains reveal their blueness, a surface adorned with blue seems to recede from our presence. Blue evokes a sense of coldness and, in turn, reminds us of shade. Rooms adorned with pure blue can appear somewhat larger, yet simultaneously empty and cold.

When blue gently merges with red, it takes on a subdued, passive character, although it retains a touch of activity. Its stimulating power, however, differs greatly from that of red-yellow. Rather than enlivening, blue-red can be said to disturb. In its more diluted state, known as lilac, it still possesses a subdued vitality, yet without a sense of gladness.

This sense of restlessness intensifies as the hue progresses, and it can be safely assumed that a carpet of pure, deep blue-red would prove intolerable.

Hence, when employed in dress, ribbons, or other ornaments, it is utilized in a lighter, more diluted form, revealing its distinct character in an exceptionally captivating manner.

Red, on the other hand, elicits a peculiar effect aligned with its unique nature. It conveys an impression of gravity, dignity, grace, and allure. These qualities manifest in its dark, deep state as well as in its light, delicate tint. Thus, the dignity of age and the charm of youth can both adorn themselves with varying degrees of this hue. Viewing a bright landscape through a red glass elicits a sense of awe-inspiring majesty.

Green, often considered the union of yellow and blue in their initial states of action, emerges as a result of their harmonious blending. The eye is met with a distinctly gratifying impression when beholding this color. When the two foundational hues are perfectly combined in equal measure, with neither overpowering the other, the eye and the mind find solace in the resulting amalgamation, perceiving it as a simple color deserving of repose.

The Experience of Color

The experiencing of colors in this manner holds great significance for the human being, particularly for the developing child. Colors are not merely external attributes or aesthetic elements; they possess deeper qualities that resonate within our soul and consciousness.

For the growing child, the encounter with colors is a vital part of their holistic development. Colors have the power to stimulate and engage the senses, awakening a heightened awareness and receptivity in the child's being. Through the vibrant hues of the world, children are offered a rich tapestry of experiences, inviting them to delve into the realms of beauty, imagination, and creativity.

> *"In the colors everything is alive. The colors are a world in themselves, and the soul element in the world of color simply cannot exist without movement; we ourselves, if we follow the colors with soul-experience, must follow with movement. People gaze open-eyed at the rainbow. But if you look at the rainbow with a little imagination, you may see there elemental beings. These elemental beings are full of activity, and they demonstrate their activity in a most remarkable manner."*
>
> *- Rudolf Steiner*

Colors play a profound role in shaping the child's relationship with the surrounding environment. They influence moods, evoke emotions, and even shape the child's perception of the world. Each color carries its own distinct qualities and energetic vibrations, which can have a profound impact on the child's inner life.

By engaging with colors through artistic activities, such as painting, drawing, and crafting, children are encouraged to develop a deeper connection with their own inner world. They learn to express their feelings, thoughts, and experiences through the language of color, cultivating a sense of self-awareness and self-expression. Artistic engagement with colors helps children to develop their imaginative faculties, fostering their ability to envision and create.

Furthermore, the encounter with colors can support the harmonious integration of body, soul, and spirit in the child. The interplay between the physical act of painting or working with colors and the inner experiences it evokes nurtures a balanced development of the child's physical and spiritual faculties. This integration is essential for the child's overall well-being and healthy growth.

In the anthroposophical understanding, colors are not viewed as mere visual stimuli but as living forces that carry spiritual qualities. They have the potential to awaken and nourish the child's inner life, fostering a sense of wonder, awe, and reverence for the world. Through the exploration of colors, children can cultivate a deeper connection with the natural world and develop a more harmonious relationship with their surroundings.

The experiencing of colors in this way is of utmost importance for the human being, particularly for the growing child. It enhances sensory perception, nurtures self-expression, fosters imaginative capacities, supports holistic development, and cultivates a deeper connection with the spiritual aspects of existence. The world of colors offers a gateway to a rich and meaningful experience of life, one that can profoundly shape and enrich the journey of the growing child.

In the early years of childhood, the boundaries between the outer and inner worlds are fluid and intertwined. Young children possess a remarkable capacity to perceive colors not merely as external attributes, but as living essences with intrinsic qualities. They feel the warmth of red and yellow, the coolness of green and blue, and sense the non-material essence that radiates from each hue.

However, as children progress in age and embark on their educational journey, a gradual shift occurs. Colors become associated solely with objects and lose their direct impact on the soul's perception. The ability to deeply feel and experience the unique qualities and effects of colors starts to wane, and the soul's eye loses its inherent vitality.

To counteract this diminishing capacity, Rudolf Steiner offers guidance to the teacher. He urges educators to create an environment where the child can continue to immerse themselves in the world of color, preserving and nurturing their innate connection to its living essence. By engaging in artistic activities, such as painting, drawing, and exploring various color mediums, the child can rekindle their capacity to feel and experience the distinct qualities and effects of colors.

Through such immersive experiences, the child's soul is invited to actively participate in the vibrant world of color, fostering a renewed sensitivity to its profound influence. This holistic engagement with color, rooted in feeling and lived experience, allows the soul's eye to develop and deepen its perception.

The teacher, therefore, becomes a guide and facilitator, creating an environment where the child can fully immerse themselves in the realm of color. By kindling the flame of inner experience and awakening the child's innate capacities, the teacher supports the ongoing development of the soul's eye, allowing it to flourish and perceive the living qualities of colors once again.

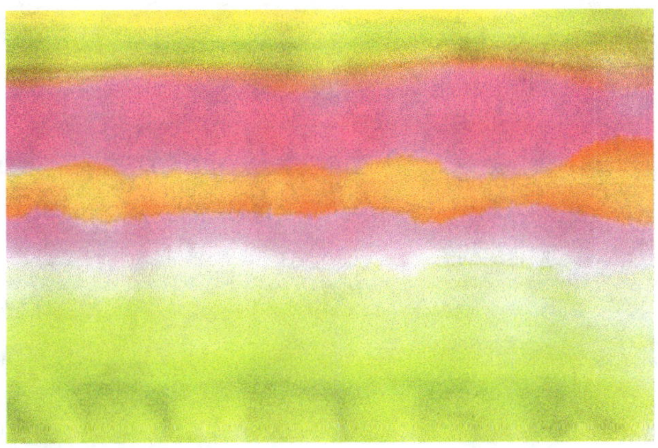

In this way, the child is offered the opportunity to maintain a vibrant and dynamic relationship with colors, transcending mere abstraction and lifeless knowledge. By nurturing the living connection between the child and the world of color, the teacher fosters the growth of the soul, enabling it to continue its journey of exploration and discovery.

Color Encounter

Another way of describing the experience of color is to say that it is an encounter with the living essence of hues. When we truly engage with colors, we go beyond the surface appearance and enter into a realm where color becomes a vibrant, dynamic presence that stirs our senses and awakens our inner being.

To experience color is to open ourselves to its qualities and effects. It is to allow color to touch us on a profound level, invoking emotional responses, evoking moods, and even influencing our perception of the world around us. It is a sensory and soulful encounter that goes beyond mere visual observation.

When we experience color, we engage with its inherent nature, feeling its warmth or coolness, its vitality or tranquility, its harmonious or disruptive energy. Colors become living entities that communicate with us, speaking a language of their own that resonates deeply within our being.

This experience of color is not limited to the visual realm alone. It reverberates through our entire being, touching our thoughts, feelings, and even physical sensations. Colors have the power to uplift, inspire, and heal, as well as to calm, soothe, and bring balance.

"The colors which the child uses for the expression of the harmonious connection with his body before the change of teeth are blue and yellow; out of these colors the soul weaves its connection with the hereditary body and transforms it. If we consider the color-combination of this last exercise we see how the soul has been led to the moment when it can free itself from too strong an attachment to forces working in the physical body (violet-black), releasing itself from intellectuality (green), and regaining the first powers with which it entered life (yellow-blue). This youthful element has become captured or is

unused; and with this free the soul can make further progress."
- From "Sleep: An Unobserved Element In Education", by Audrey E. Mc Allen

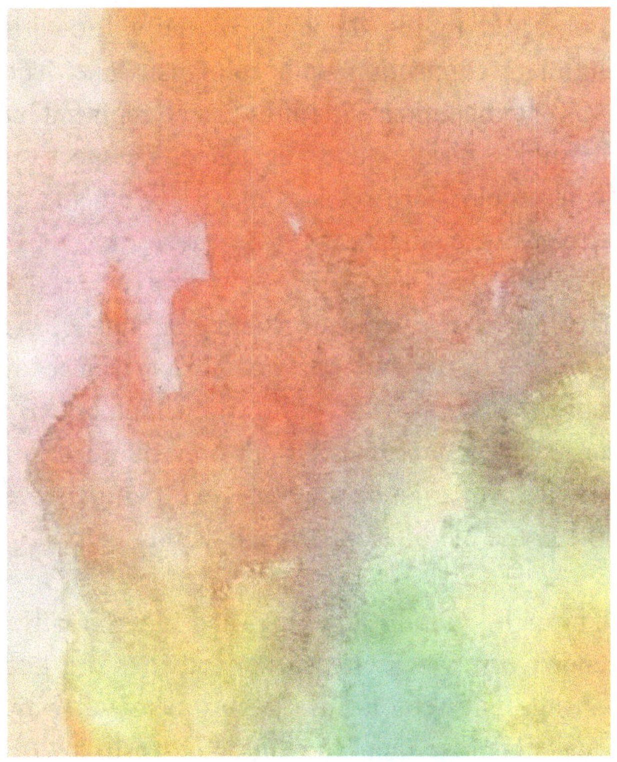

In the world of the growing child, the experience of color is particularly significant. Young children have a natural affinity for colors, sensing their qualities and responding to their effects with a heightened sensitivity.

They perceive colors not as separate entities but as vibrant expressions of life that engage their whole being.

However, as children mature and become immersed in the demands of daily life, this intimate connection with color can fade. The vibrant encounter with hues can be replaced by a more distant and detached perspective, where colors are seen as mere adornments or decorative elements.

It is our task, as educators and guardians of the soul, to foster and nurture the experience of color throughout the child's development. By creating environments and opportunities for immersive artistic activities, we can reignite the flame of color experience within them.

Through painting, drawing, and other creative endeavors, we invite children to explore and engage with colors in a deeply personal way. We encourage them to feel the brushstrokes, to immerse themselves in the interplay of hues, and to let color express their innermost thoughts and emotions.

In this way, we awaken the child's capacity to experience color as a living presence once again. We help them rediscover the magic and wonder of colors, allowing them to reestablish a vibrant and meaningful relationship with the world of hues.

By fostering the experience of color, we support the child's holistic development, nurturing their imagination, emotional intelligence, and aesthetic sensibilities. We enable them to perceive the world with fresh eyes, imbuing their lives with a deeper sense of beauty, meaning, and connectedness.

The experience of color, therefore, becomes a transformative journey, an ongoing exploration of the living tapestry of hues that surrounds us. It is an invitation to embrace the richness and depth of the world of color, and to allow its vibrant presence to illuminate our path of self-discovery and growth.

Rudolf Steiner and the Waldorf approach build upon Goethe's insights, recognizing the profound impact that colors have on our inner world. Beyond their visual attributes, colors possess a spiritual quality that speaks directly to the soul, evoking feelings and stirring impulses of will.

When children are introduced to colors in a holistic and conscious manner, they can experience the depths of emotions that arise in response to each hue. Through artistic activities and thoughtful guidance, we can guide children to engage with colors in a way that allows them to spontaneously connect with the inner life and shades of feeling that colors evoke.

Just as Goethe observed, red carries a certain challenge, a fiery intensity that arouses the soul. It ignites passion, stirs our courage, and beckons us to take action. By immersing children in the presence of red and facilitating their exploration of this vibrant hue, we enable them to experience its moral effect and its power to awaken their will forces.

On the other hand, blue holds a different quality, one of stillness and contemplation. It has the ability to quiet the soul, inviting moments of introspection and inner calm. When children are surrounded by blue and encouraged to engage with its serene presence, they can naturally attune themselves to its tranquilizing effect and feel a sense of inner peace and harmony.

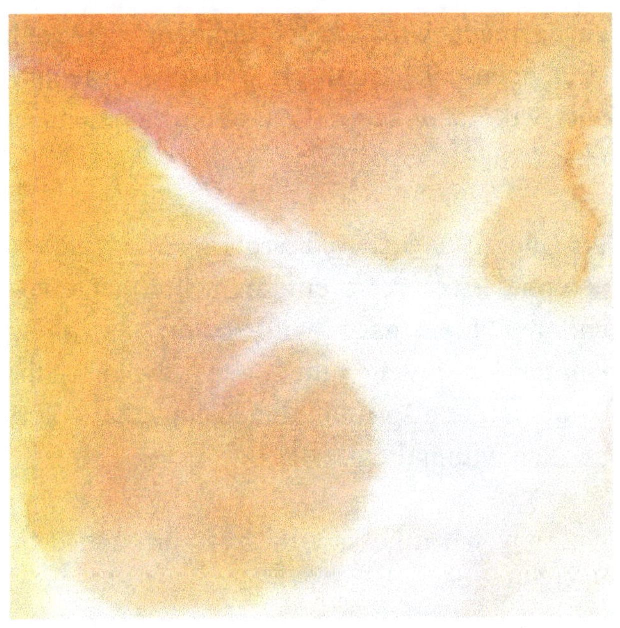

The Waldorf approach recognizes that colors are not passive entities but living beings with a profound spiritual essence. Even blind individuals, who may not perceive colors through their physical sight, can still experience the moral effects and inner life of colors through their heightened sensitivity to the spiritual realms.

By presenting colors to children in a conscious and meaningful way, we can nurture their capacity to feel the vibrant interplay of hues and recognize the deep relationship between color and human experience. This conscious engagement with colors enlivens the soul, strengthens the connection between feeling and will, and supports the development of moral impulses.

In the Waldorf classroom and artistic activities, we create environments that invite children to engage with colors as living entities, allowing them to explore the emotional and spiritual dimensions that colors awaken within them.

One boy when he saw the red surrounded by the blue said:

"My Red is having a rest, he's lying down in the blue bed."

Another child exclaimed with satisfaction after painting the blue over with red:

"Now the Red has swallowed up the Blue."

A four-and-a-half-year-old girl cried out happily while painting:

"My Orange is so happy it wants to jump everywhere."

Through these experiences, children develop a profound relationship with colors, cultivating their aesthetic sensibilities, moral discernment, and imaginative capacities.

For older children, a deep appreciation for colors and painting emerges, as they engage in the artistic process with a sense of quietude and observation. They paint attentively, observing the interplay between colors on the paper, noting how one color encounters another—containing, joining, or giving rise to new hues. They also become attuned to the emergence of forms that take shape within their paintings.

With their imaginative faculties ignited, they perceive a multitude of images and scenes within their artwork, as if unlocking hidden worlds and narratives through the play of colors.

In the Waldorf approach, we honor and encourage this natural inclination of the child to explore colors freely, allowing them to follow their own formative forces in their artistic endeavors. Children delight in setting colors beside each other, not with a specific intent or meaning, but guided by an instinctive purpose. They develop a remarkable instinct for color placement, intuitively discovering harmonious combinations and creating vibrant compositions.

When children engage in watercolor painting, we discern two distinct approaches unfolding in the first strokes of their brushes.

Some children begin by creating individual patches of color, placing additional patches of the same or different hues adjacent to or atop the initial ones. Alternatively, they might distribute the subsequent patches across the entire expanse of the paper.

Other children, on the other hand, embark on a process of "painting" lines and forms, which they subsequently fill in with color, employing the brush much like a pencil.

While the former group naturally merges with the process of painting, flowing effortlessly and intuitively with the brush's movements, the latter group often approaches the act of painting more analytically. They tend to rely less on direct experiences of colors and find it challenging to immerse themselves fully in the playful dance of hues.

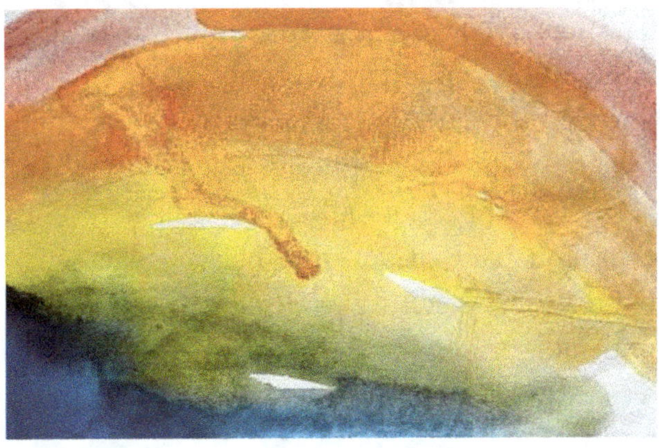

For these children, we gladly offer gentle guidance, providing hints and suggestions that help them delve deeper into the realms of color. We support them in discovering the joy and richness that can be found in the dynamic interactions of colors, encouraging them to explore and embrace the vibrant possibilities that unfold before their eyes.

In this way, older children continue to cultivate their artistic skills, while also deepening their connection to the transformative and expressive qualities of colors. Their artistic endeavors become a source of personal exploration and growth, fostering their capacity for observation, imagination, and harmonious engagement with the world of colors.

Through their journey of painting and color exploration, children not only develop their artistic abilities but also nurture essential faculties of perception, sensitivity, and aesthetic appreciation. They embark on a profound path of self-discovery and creative expression, fostering a lifelong relationship with colors and the transformative power of artistic engagement.

By embracing the teachings of Goethe and integrating them into our educational practices, we help children develop a deep appreciation for the moral effects of colors. We empower them to navigate the rich tapestry of hues, inspiring them to bring forth their innermost qualities and engage with the world in a conscious and compassionate way.

'People who can see are wrong when they think that blind people are excluded from all the beauty of color. And the blind author Ursula Burkhard describes how she was able to form differentiated concepts of color, particularly with regard to fairy tales, and how she learned to experience inwardly the essence of the colors. Simple folk tales said more to me about colors. When Snow White's wicked stepmother turned yellow with envy it must have been a poisonous yellow, different from the good nourishing yellow of ears of corn. And in how many moods does the color red live in 'Snow White and Rose Red'! There is the delicate red of the blossom on the rosebush and the living red of the berries in the wood. Wicked red blazes out of the face of the angry dwarf. The red sky of the morning shines with promise over the precipice where all night long the guardian angel watched over the children who had tarried in the woods. In the redemptory red of the evening the king's

son is released from his bear shape, and now we can see him living as a king entirely in red, and wearing, instead of the black rough fur, the mantle of purple-red, the red that is august and regal."

- *Hellen Keller*

Color in Fairy Tales

Through fairy tales, children encounter colors in a profound and intimate way, forging deep associations with the hues that populate these enchanting stories. These tales weave vivid imagery and symbolism, where colors take on significant meaning, capturing the imagination and stirring the hearts of young listeners.

In the Waldorf approach, this love of color finds further expression through the artistic medium of watercolor painting. At the ages of four and five, children are drawn to the vibrant palette of watercolors, exploring the individual colors in their nuanced variations. Each color carries its own essence, evoking different moods and qualities, and children become attuned to the unique character of each hue.

As children engage in the process of painting, they are enlivened by the colors and captivated by the unfolding magic on their paper. Their delight and enthusiasm overflow, and they yearn to share their color-filled experiences with their peers, siblings, and parents. They eagerly express their observations and insights, engaging in lively discussions about their paintings and the interplay of colors.

One can hear their vibrant comments and narratives: "My Red is engaged in a fierce battle with the Blue, and he triumphs as the stronger force, pushing the Blue aside." (In their artwork, the dominance of the red hue might have covered most of the blue, leaving only a small strip visible.)

Through these creative encounters, children not only refine their artistic skills but also deepen their connection to the language of colors. They learn to perceive the dynamic relationships between colors, experiencing the interplay of light and darkness, warmth and coolness, strength and subtlety. Their artistic endeavors become a source of personal expression, where they can communicate their inner world and engage with the world of colors in a lively and imaginative way.

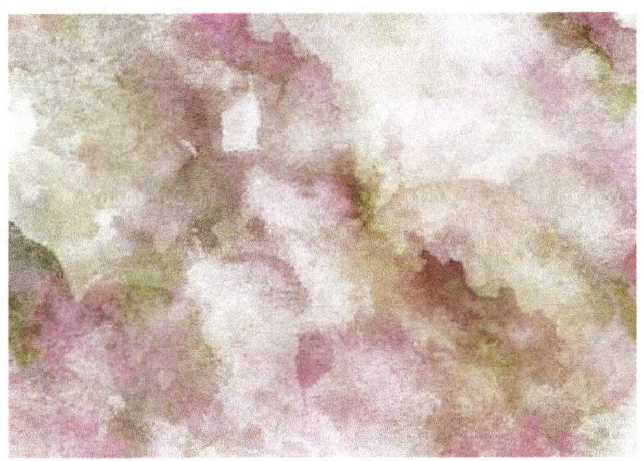

In the nurturing environment of the Waldorf classroom, children are encouraged to explore the depths of color, celebrating the unique qualities and interactions of each hue. This formative experience kindles their aesthetic sensibilities, fosters their imaginative capacities, and nurtures their ability to appreciate the intricacies and harmonies of the color realm.

Through their encounters with colors in fairy tales and their artistic explorations, children develop a profound relationship with the world of colors. This relationship becomes a wellspring of inspiration, fostering their creativity, empathy, and ability to perceive the subtleties and beauty in the tapestry of life.

Preparing to Paint

Preparing for watercolor painting holds a special place unlike other mediums such as colored pencils, chalk, crayons, or wax. It encompasses a vital process that requires thoughtful readiness and is especially significant for children as active participants in the art form.

With great enthusiasm, children eagerly join in the preparatory tasks. They joyfully assist in filling the water jars, observing with fascination as the colors dissolve gradually in the water, carefully blending them with their brushes.

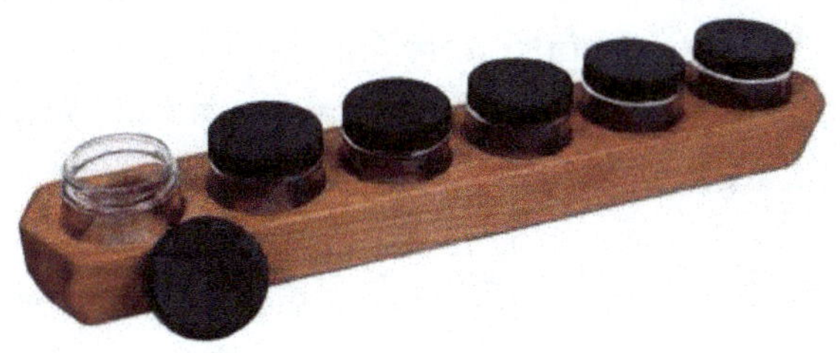

They attentively follow each step, including rinsing the brushes in the water, witnessing the magical emergence of captivating hues. Their immersion in the enchanting unfolding of the color process is palpable.

As their anticipation builds, they eagerly await the moment to begin painting. However, before diving into their artistic exploration, there is a crucial step to be taken—preparing the paper. Here, too, children can actively engage with eagerness. Even younger children can participate in each stage of the preparation process, offering them a sense of involvement and ownership.

Through collaborative efforts, children develop a deep connection and appreciation for the art they are about to create. They witness firsthand the intricate interplay between materials and artistic expression. This participatory approach not only cultivates a sense of responsibility but also nurtures their reverence for the materials and the artistic process itself.

By involving children in the preparation of painting materials, we honor their innate desire for active engagement. They not only gain a sense of agency but also develop an acute awareness of the materials' significance and the intricate relationships between colors and the artistic outcome.

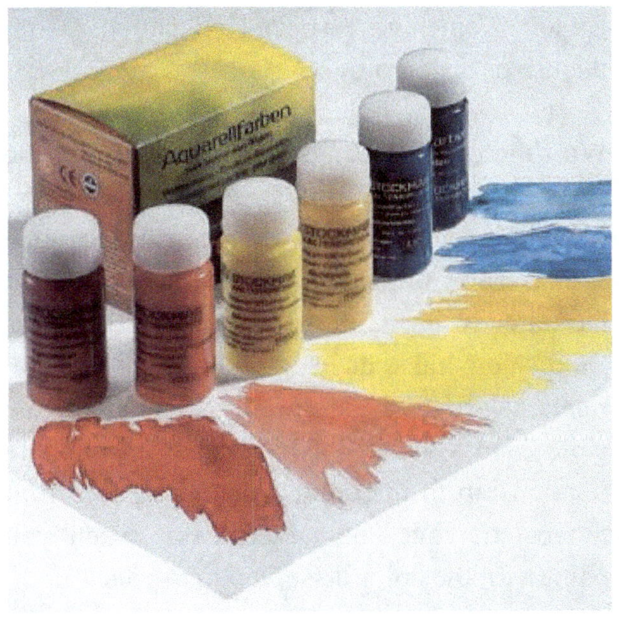

Through this meaningful involvement, children forge a profound bond with the artistic process, fostering their attention to detail, creativity, and appreciation for the harmonious intermingling of colors and materials. Their contributions to the preparatory phase become an integral part of their artistic journey, enriching their experiences and deepening their connection to the captivating world of watercolor painting.

In "*Painting with Children*", by Brunhild Muller, it states:

Rudolf Steiner gave special indications about the use of watercolors:

We should be especially careful not to let the children use paints straight out of a paintbox. That is wrong even in artistic painting. One should paint out of the dish where the paint has already been mixed with water or other fluid. You must develop an inward intimate relationship to the color - and so must the child- and you do not have such an intimate relationship to the color when you paint from the palette, but you develop this when you paint with the color dissolved in the dish."

Painting Steps

The preparation for the painting process in the Waldorf approach follows a deliberate and mindful sequence. By honoring the materials and considering the child's engagement, we lay the foundation for a meaningful artistic experience.

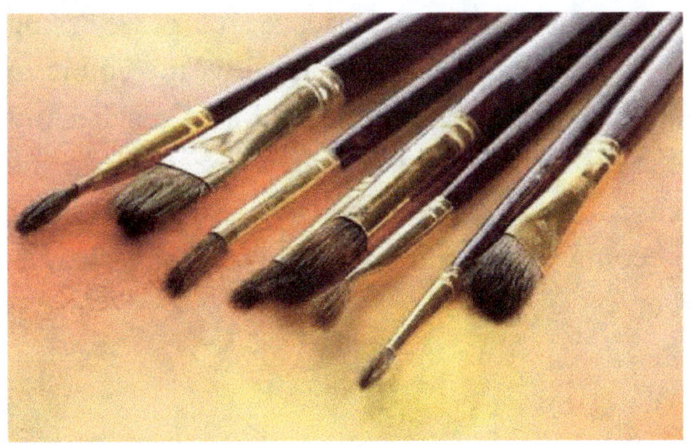

Here are the steps to prepare for painting:

Mixing the color:

Begin by selecting watercolor paints from tubes. With a fine hair brush designated for mixing purposes, blend each color in separate pots or glass jars. The recommended ratio is one part paint to two parts water. Stir gently while gradually adding water until the desired dilution is achieved. To test the color intensity, use a damp piece of paper. Please note that yellow may require more paint than red, while blue can maintain a proportion of one to two.

Distribution:

Once the colors are mixed, distribute them into small dishes, bowls, saucers, or lids. For a truly enchanting experience, consider using little glass jars or pots that allow the colors to shine beautifully for the children. Each child should receive one pot of each color. In the case of two children who are capable of keeping their colors clean, they may share a pot.

Water jars:

Fill jam jars about three-quarters full of water to serve as containers for cleaning brushes. Each child should have at least one glass for water, as it tends to become soiled quickly during the painting process.

Preparing the paper:

There are two recommended methods for preparing the paper. The first involves dipping the paper into a large dish, photo tray, or basin of water, ensuring that it absorbs the water evenly. Alternatively, lay the paper on a painting board or table and gently wipe it with a wet sponge, preferably a natural sponge.

This wiping motion should be performed from side to side, top to bottom, or from the center outward—avoid circular motions to prevent roughening of the paper. Turn the paper over and repeat the process on the other side. Carefully remove excess water by using the sponge to soak it up and smooth out any bubbles or kinks. This step is vital to achieve a proper painting surface. The size of the paper should be suitable for the child's capabilities but should be at least A4 (12" x 8"). The paper can be laid flat on the table or on a board, and any paint that touches the table's edge can be easily wiped away with a damp cloth.

Readiness:

Only after completing the aforementioned steps should the child receive a brush and a cloth. The cloth is used to wipe the brush and squeeze out any excess water or paint, ensuring the right consistency for painting.

Additionally, here are some recommendations regarding equipment:

Choose broad, flat hair brushes in sizes 16 or 18. These brushes allow for delicate application of paint and facilitate layering more easily compared to bristle brushes.

Opt for white drawing paper over drawing block paper, as the latter tends to contain higher levels of lime, making it less absorbent for watercolors.

Rudolf Steiner gave specific indications about the use of watercolors:

"We should be especially careful not to let the children use paints straight out of a paint box. That is wrong even in artistic painting. One should paint out of the dish where the paint has already been mixed with water or other fluid. You must develop an inward intimate relationship to the color - and so must the child - and you do not have such an intimate relationship to the color when you paint from

the palette, but you develop this when you paint with the color dissolved in the dish."

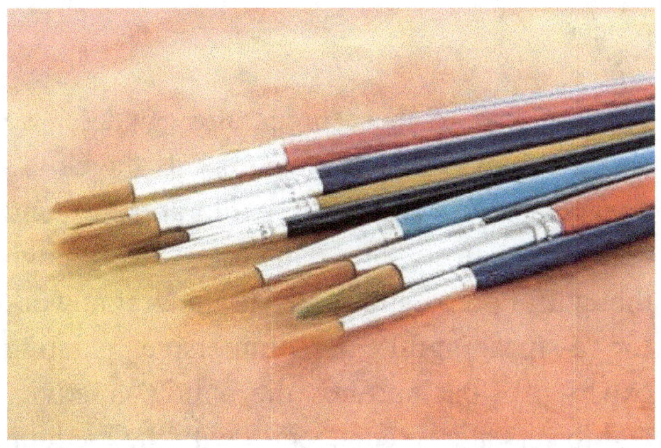

Once the preparations have been meticulously attended to, a sense of anticipation settles among the children, creating an atmosphere of quiet expectancy.

With this air of reverence, the brush is gently dipped into the jar of water, ensuring its cleanliness. It is then pressed against the cloth, allowing any excess water to be absorbed. The next step is to carefully dip the brush into the color pot, where the chosen hue awaits.

Before bringing the brush to the paper, it is important to gently wipe it two or three times along the edge of the pot. This careful act ensures that the paint application will not be overly saturated or too wet, allowing for greater control and precision in the painting process.

By attending to these preparatory details, we create an environment that supports the child's engagement, artistic exploration, and reverence for the materials. Through thoughtful preparation, we lay the groundwork for a meaningful and immersive painting experience that nurtures the child's creativity and fosters a deep connection with the medium of watercolors.

Painting the Colors

Engaging in the act of painting with a vibrant palette of colors, such as red, blue, green, yellow, orange, violet, brown, white, gray, and black, offers us a unique opportunity to intimately acquaint ourselves with the distinctive qualities of each hue.

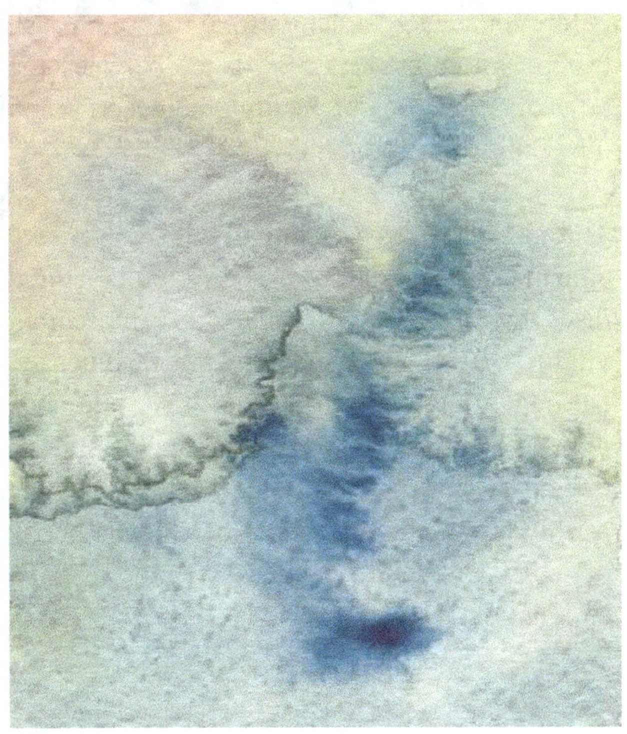

Painting with colors is not merely an external activity; it is a profound experience of coexistence and immersion within their essence.

As we delicately apply these colors to the canvas or paper, we enter into a living relationship with them. We surrender ourselves to their captivating presence, allowing their inherent qualities to unfold before our eyes. Each stroke of the brush becomes a conversation, a dance between the artist and the colors, revealing their secrets and unveiling their truths.

Through the act of painting with colors, we embark on a journey of exploration and discovery. We come to understand the vibrant vitality of red, the tranquil depth of blue, the harmonious growth of green, the luminous radiance of yellow, the fiery passion of orange, the mysterious enchantment of violet, the earthly grounding of brown, the ethereal purity of white, the subtle nuances of gray, and the enigmatic power of black.

In this artistic communion, we transcend the mere surface level of observation and enter into a realm where colors become our companions, our guides, and our sources of inspiration. Painting with colors becomes a means of perceiving the world, not only with our physical senses but also with the depth of our soul.

Rainer Maria Rilke wrote about Cezanne as follows:

"Never has it been so apparent that painting is really an activity that goes on among the colors themselves that the colors must be left alone to sort themselves out Painting is the intercourse between the colors themselves and if anyone interferes by imposing on them his

own arrangement, or allows any human consideration, or his own ingenuity, pre-selection, or mental dexterity to have any say at all in the matter, then the colors will be disturbed and disorientated in their interaction."

As we live with and in the colors, we cultivate a profound connection to the diverse facets of existence. We learn to navigate the intricate interplay of light and shade, of warmth and coolness, of vibrant intensity and serene subtlety. Through this intimate engagement with colors, we develop a heightened sensitivity to their nuances and the profound impact they have on our inner being.

Painting with colors becomes a transformative experience, an invitation to embrace the kaleidoscope of life's hues and to express our inner world through their vibrant language. It is an act of creation, of self-discovery, and of communion with the spiritual essence that permeates all things.

As we introduce children to the interplay of colors, we provide them with the tools and knowledge to explore their own artistic expression. We offer them examples and demonstrations, not as strict templates to be replicated, but as sources of inspiration from which they can freely draw. It is through this process of observation, emulation, and individual interpretation that children become fully engaged in their own unique artistic endeavors.

The magical encounter between blue and red, for instance, manifests differently in each child's artwork. The colors themselves possess a dynamic relationship, an inherent harmony or contrast that beckons to be explored. Guided by their own intuitive understanding, children of even preschool age can unleash the captivating interaction of colors within their paintings.

While we may present our own artwork as a point of reference, it is crucial to emphasize that children should not be confined to slavish imitation. Instead, we encourage them to follow their own creative instincts and to infuse their work with their own individuality. This fosters a deep sense of engagement, allowing them to immerse themselves fully in the artistic process.

In this way, children discover the joy of artistic exploration and self-expression. They develop a genuine connection with the colors, as they witness the magic unfold on their own canvases. Each brushstroke, each blending of hues, carries their unique imprint, reflecting their inner world and their personal interpretation of the colors' interplay.

As educators and guides, we create a nurturing environment that encourages children to tap into their innate creative potential. We foster an atmosphere where they can freely explore the realm of color, where their imaginations can soar, and where their artistic voices can be heard. Through this process, children not only engage with the colors themselves but also cultivate their own inner world of creativity, self-expression, and wonder.

Now let us see how these thoughts find a practical application in our painting with children.

Already while mixing the colors, I give the children indications of what we are going to paint, rather like this:

"Blue and Red are going to work magic on each other today" or "I wonder what Yellow is going to tell Blue" or if we are going to paint only with blue, "today Blue wants to be alone" or if we are going to paint with only two red colors the dark carmine and light vermilion, "Two red brothers made a bet, who would be the stronger yet."

With our intentional guidance and inspiration, we can guide children along a path that leads them to the enchanting world of color. Our ultimate goal is to awaken and nurture their innate creativity, allowing it to flourish and unfold.

During one of our painting sessions, we embarked on a delightful adventure entitled "Blue, Yellow, and Orange Are Going to Play Together."

The children eagerly dipped their brushes into a little bit of blue, a touch of yellow, and a hint of orange, and carefully applied these vibrant hues onto their papers. Each child approached the canvas with their own unique vision. One child chose to place all three colors side by side in the center of the sheet, while another scattered them in separate corners, and yet another playfully scattered patches of color throughout the paper.

As the painting unfolded, the individuality of each child's creative expression became evident. In the accompanying picture, you can still perceive the boy's initial strokes of bright yellow and radiant orange, deliberately leaving spaces for the insertion of blue. The artwork radiates a sense of liveliness and movement, almost as if the colors themselves are engaged in their own playful dance.

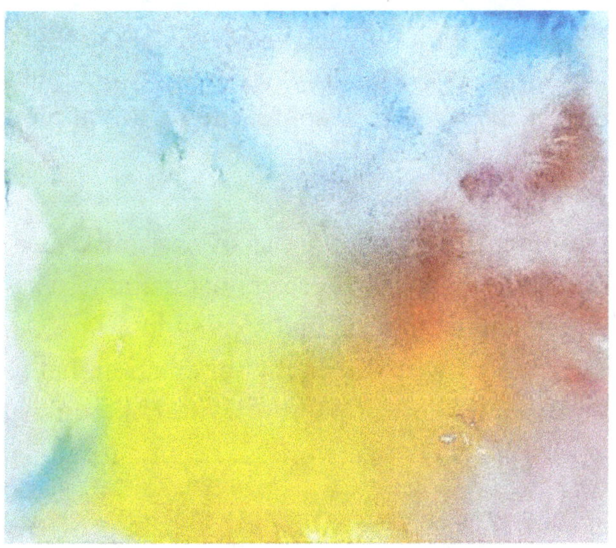

In this shared experience, the colors not only come alive on the paper but also within the hearts and imaginations of the children. Each brushstroke, each carefully placed hue, contributes to the overall dynamism of the artwork. The picture becomes a testament to the children's engagement with the colors, inviting us to witness the magic and joy that unfold when young hearts and minds interact with the world of art.

Through such creative explorations, children not only develop their artistic skills but also cultivate their capacity for imagination, self-expression, and individuality. They learn to navigate the vibrant interplay of colors, allowing them to discover their own unique perspectives and approaches to artistic creation.

Through the colors, we discover a universe of possibilities, where our imagination takes flight, our emotions find expression, and our soul dances with the rhythm of creation. Let us embrace the gift of painting with colors, for it opens the doors to a world of beauty, meaning, and profound connection.

The Language of Watercolors

Children who delight in the world of painting and coloring always seem to have an insatiable appetite for paper. Their artistic creations flow effortlessly and swiftly onto the page, leaving them yearning for more. It may seem peculiar, then, to consider providing a young child of three or four years with 100% rag content watercolor paper for their painting endeavors.

However, the true value lies in the opportunity to embark on a special journey of color exploration together, not only in the experience itself but also in the beauty that often emerges in their artworks.

To engage in this enchanting process, we can begin by acquiring just three tubes of watercolor paint: red, yellow, and blue. These primary colors will serve as the foundation for all the paintings that will come to life. Remarkably, even a small amount of paint goes a long way, and these tubes will last indefinitely, accompanying the child on their artistic adventures.

In terms of paper, we can opt for inexpensive medium-textured watercolor paper. To make it more manageable for young hands, large sheets can be cut into four smaller ones. Prior to painting, it is important to soak the paper in water for approximately 30 minutes, allowing it to absorb the moisture and prepare itself for the forthcoming creative expressions.

While the paper soaks, we can proceed to mix the paints in small containers with lids, such as repurposed baby food jars. Adding two tablespoons (30 ml) of water to a small amount of watercolor paint squeezed from the tube, we create the perfect consistency for painting. Thoroughly mixing the paint ensures a harmonious blend of color.

Each young painter will require a bowl of water, a damp sponge or rag, and a wide watercolor brush. These tools will accompany them on their artistic journey, facilitating the exploration of colors and the application of paint onto the awaiting canvas.

Once the paper has soaked and absorbed the water, it can be carefully placed on a smooth, flat surface. It is important to avoid the formation of air bubbles during this process, but if any do arise, a gentle touch of the sponge or cloth will smooth them away, ensuring a pristine surface for the creative adventure to unfold.

Those who possess a penchant for expressive brushwork and enjoy the act of drawing with a paintbrush can be encouraged to explore a freer approach by gripping the brush with the same fluidity as a house painter would. Much of the magic happens when the brush lifts from the paper, allowing the colors to gracefully spread across the wet surface, sometimes mingling with other hues to birth a harmonious third shade. Remember to cleanse the brush by rinsing it in cold water before dipping it into a new color, ensuring the purity and integrity of each hue.

Never Hang to Dry!

Once the paintings are complete, they should be laid flat to dry. It is crucial to avoid hanging them prematurely, as this may disrupt the delicate balance of colors and lead to undesirable effects.

After each painting session, brushes should be thoroughly rinsed clean with cold water. The leftover paints can be safely stored for future artistic endeavors, ensuring their longevity and providing opportunities for continuous exploration.

The showcased paintings depicted in this collection exemplify the captivating outcomes achieved through the practice of painting with watercolors on wet paper. However, as the stack of completed artworks grows, finding adequate space on the refrigerator or walls becomes a delightful challenge.

To bestow a second life upon these cherished pieces, we can engage in exercises of imagination and economy. Even in paintings that may appear unremarkable as a whole, hidden treasures often reside in sections where the colors intermingle beautifully.

These sections can be carefully cut out and repurposed to create an array of delightful crafts, such as birthday invitations, place cards, gift wrappings, book covers, and even whimsical crowns. Additionally, the sturdy watercolor paper lends itself well to the art of origami, the ancient Japanese practice of paper folding. With its strength and resilience, it can be skillfully fashioned into windmills, boxes, and a myriad of other captivating shapes.

Through this process of repurposing and transforming, the child's creativity is further nurtured, encouraging them to see beauty and potential in even the seemingly ordinary. It fosters a sense of resourcefulness and appreciation for the artistic journey, where every stroke and every color holds the promise of new possibilities.

Summary of Directions:

- Purchase three tubes of watercolor paint: red, yellow, and blue.
- These three colors will be used for all the paintings.
- A small amount of paint is sufficient for each painting, making the tubes last indefinitely.
- Use inexpensive medium textured watercolor paper.
- Cut large sheets into four smaller sheets for painting.
- Soak the paper in water for 30 minutes.
- Mix the paints in small containers with lids, such as baby food jars.
- Add 2 tablespoons (30 ml) of water to approximately 5-10 mm (1/4 - 1/2 inch) of watercolor paint squeezed from the tube.

- Mix the paint thoroughly.
- Provide each painter with a bowl of water, a damp sponge or rag, and a wide watercolor brush.
- After soaking the paper, place it on a smooth flat surface, ensuring there are no air bubbles. Use a sponge or cloth to smooth out any remaining bubbles.

Color Stories

Sometimes, as we prepare for the painting, I share a little color story with the children:

Once upon a time, Yellow went on a search for Blue. "Oh, there you are! I've been looking for you," exclaimed Yellow joyfully. They laughed and embraced each other tightly, so happy to be reunited. Their joy was so immense that they transformed into the color of lush green grass.

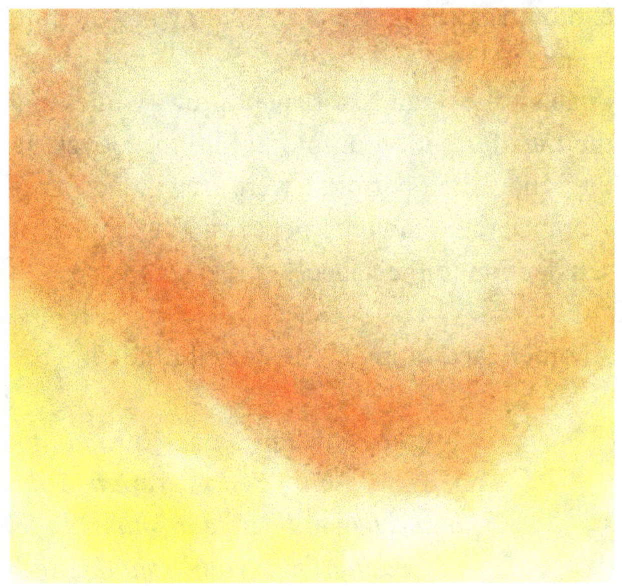

Guided by this enchanting story, the children eagerly began their painting journey. With Prussian blue and lemon yellow on their brushes, they carefully created a large yellow patch along the top edge of the paper and a smaller blue patch at the bottom. Then, they skillfully brought the yellow down towards the blue and the blue up towards the yellow, repeating the motion several times. As the colors intertwined, the yellow enveloped the blue, merging and blending harmoniously.

Initially, the strokes were gentle, gradually gaining strength and intensity. The children explored layering the colors, allowing them to intermingle and overlap. With each brushstroke, their excitement grew, witnessing the transformation unfold before their eyes. In the end, their efforts were rewarded as a vibrant green hue emerged, bringing smiles of satisfaction to their faces.

Another captivating color story unfolded:

A bright glowing Red and a radiantly shining Yellow were friends.
'I should like to be able to shine out as radiantly as you,' said the Red.
'And I should like to glow as brightly as you,'

said the Yellow.
Then Yellow gave Red some of the radiant shining and Red gave Yellow some of his bright glowing.

Inspired by this tale, the children embarked on their own artistic journey, painting with enthusiasm and curiosity. They embraced the vibrant Red and radiant Yellow, intertwining their colors on the canvas. With each brushstroke, they celebrated the harmonious blending of these hues, cherishing the beauty that emerged from their creative exploration.

In this way, the stories served as an imaginative guide, allowing the children to connect deeply with the colors and infuse their paintings with their own unique expressions.

Another Story to Share...

Once upon a time, in a realm where colors danced and played, there existed a graceful and serene Blue and a vibrant and lively Orange. These two colors, though distinct, admired the qualities that each possessed. Blue yearned to emit the fiery energy of Orange, while Orange longed for the tranquil aura of Blue.

One fateful day, they decided to embark on a transformative journey. Standing face to face, they began their enchanting dance, swirling and twirling in perfect harmony. With each graceful movement, their colors intertwined, merging and blending in a mesmerizing display.

In the midst of their dance, a magical alchemy occurred. Blue absorbed the vivacity of Orange, infusing it with its own peaceful nature. Orange, in turn, embraced the serenity of Blue, infusing it with its fiery spirit. Together, they birthed a new hue, a majestic and enchanting color—Majestic Purple.

We can delve deep into the realm of colors and explore their relationships by celebrating the birthdays of red, yellow, or blue. When it was time to honor blue on its special day, the children gathered with their brushes and paint palettes, ready to immerse themselves in the enchanting world of this serene hue.

Blue took center stage as the birthday color, and the children began their painting process by adorning their paper solely with shades of blue. They were so captivated by the allure of blue that they almost forgot to leave space for the other colors to join the celebration.

However, the wise teacher gently guided the children, encouraging them to embark on a new color experience imbued with rhythm. With each brushstroke, they explored the harmonious interplay between blue and the other hues, discovering the wondrous dance of colors that unfolded before their eyes.

As they embraced the rhythm of the painting process, the children intuitively understood that the essence of blue was enriched when it mingled and intertwined with other colors. They blended hues together, creating exquisite variations and harmonies, expanding their artistic horizons beyond the initial dominance of blue.

Through this colorful journey, the children discovered the magic of balance and cooperation among the colors. They learned that while blue deserved its moment in the spotlight, its true radiance was enhanced when it embraced the vibrant presence of its fellow hues.

In the end, the paintings that emerged from the birthday celebration of blue reflected the beauty of unity and the joy of artistic exploration. The children had experienced a profound connection with the colors, unlocking their creative potential and witnessing the transformative power of harmonious collaboration.

And now unto the party sped
Two new guests, Yellow and Red.

Now the children brought in plenty of yellow and added the red, and the rhyme went on:

They bring as is on birthdays
Their special presents to the Blue
They give a cloak, they give a rug

To wrap the Blue up warm and snug.

Then the children painted the red and yellow into the blue. But while they took care not to cover the birthday color completely their interest was directed much more to the new colors that had been coming about, green, orange and violet.

Then Blue cried out, 'What's happened here?
Orange and Green did soon appear,
and Violet too, come stand by me!
And be my friends, you colors three!

Verses hold a special place in setting the mood for painting. Prior to the artistic exploration, I share the essence of the verses, igniting the spark of imagination within each child. Throughout the painting process, the words dance in their hearts, waiting patiently for the perfect moment to be recited.

And now, as the paintings near completion, the time has come to give voice to the verses. With a gentle voice, I recite the lines, intertwining the magical realm of words with the vivid colors on the paper. The children listen attentively, their spirits soaring with the lyrical flow.

With the final stanza of the verses, the painting session gracefully comes to an end. The children, filled with a sense of accomplishment and wonder, gaze upon their masterpieces with awe and satisfaction. The verses linger in the air, infusing the room with a sense of poetic beauty and artistic fulfillment.

As the children bid farewell to the painting session, they carry the essence of the verses within their hearts, forever intertwined with their colorful creations. The journey of art and verse continues to inspire them, sparking their creativity and nurturing their souls.

With these heartfelt verses, I conclude the painting session. The children, brimming with the wonders they had witnessed and the creations they had brought to life, tidied up their painting supplies, their hearts filled with joy. As they put away their brushes and palettes, the melodic rhythm of the verses echoed in their minds, embracing them with its enchanting cadence.

Verses to Stimulate Painting

Using verses to stimulate young artists is a powerful and enchanting approach that enhances their painting experiences. These carefully crafted verses serve as catalysts for imagination, inviting children to delve into the world of colors and create artwork infused with magic and wonder.

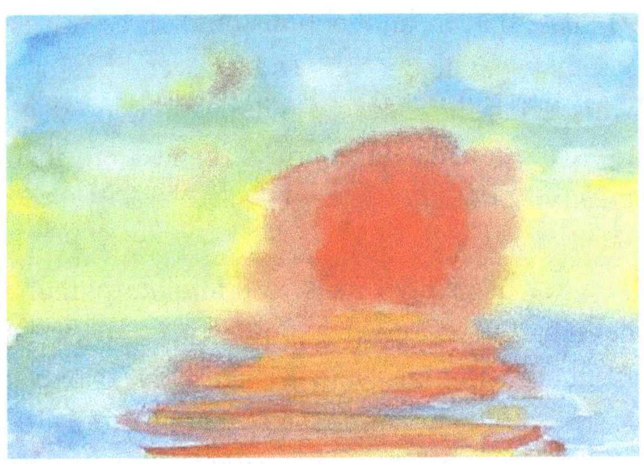

By incorporating verses into the painting process, children are not only engaged in a visual exploration but also in a multisensory and immersive experience. The rhythmic flow of the verses ignites their auditory senses, setting the tone for their artistic journey. As they listen to the verses, their minds are transported to vivid landscapes, vibrant scenes, and whimsical characters, sparking their imagination and fueling their creative expression.

Verses act as gentle guides, offering imagery and descriptive language that inspire young artists to visualize and interpret colors in unique ways. They evoke emotions, create narratives, and stimulate curiosity, providing a framework for children to explore the interplay of hues, shades, and textures on their canvases. As they paint, the verses act as companions, whispering in their ears and encouraging them to experiment, take risks, and let their creativity flow.

The act of using verses to stimulate painting cultivates a deep connection between language, rhythm, and visual expression. It fosters a holistic approach to art, where words and colors intertwine, creating a symbiotic relationship. Children not only engage with the verses intellectually but also emotionally, as they embody the essence of the words in their brushstrokes, bringing the verses to life on their canvases.

The use of verses provides a sense of structure and narrative, anchoring children's painting experiences in a meaningful context. It allows them to weave stories, evoke moods, and convey messages through their artwork. The verses become an integral part of their creative process, serving as a source of inspiration and a reflection of their artistic journey.

Using verses to stimulate young artists expands their artistic horizons and nurtures their imaginative capabilities. It encourages them to explore the boundless possibilities of colors and storytelling, instilling a sense of wonder and enchantment in their artistic endeavors. By integrating verses into the painting process, educators and parents can unlock the full potential of children's creativity and provide them with a transformative and magical artistic experience.

Below are a few of our personal favorites which we shared on Waldorf Homeschoolers.

My Lady Spring

My Lady Spring is dressed in green,
She wears a primrose crown,
And little baby buds and twigs

Are clinging to her gown;
The sun shines if she laughs at all,
But if she weeps the raindrops fall.

Violets

I know, blue modest violets
Gleaming with dew at morn
I know the place you come from
And the way that you are born!
When God cast holes in heaven
The holes the stars look through
He let the scraps tall down to earth
The little scraps are you

Spring

Now daisies pied, and violets blue,
And lady smocks all silver white,
And cuckoo buds of yellow hue
Do paint the meadows with delight.
The cuckoo now on every tree
Sings cuckoo, cuckoo

0 Dandelion

'0 dandelion, yellow as gold,
What do you do all day?'
I just wait here in the tall green grass

Till the children come to play.'
'0 dandelion, yellow as gold,
What do you do all night?'
I wait and wait till the cool dews fall
And my hair grows long and white.'
'And what do you do when your hair is white
And the children come to play?'
'They take me up in their dimpled hands
And blow my hair away!'

White Sheep

White sheep, white sheep
On a blue hill,
When the wind stops
You all stand still.
You all run away
When the winds blow;
White sheep, white sheep,
Where do you go?

Red in Autumn

Tipperty-toes, the smallest elf,
Sat on a mushroom by himself,
Playing a little tinkling tune
Under the big round harvest moon;
And this is the song that Tipperty made
To sing to the little tune he played

'Red are the hips, red are the haws,
Red and gold are the leaves that fall,
Red are the poppies in the corn,
Red berries on the rowan tall;
Red is the big round harvest moon,
And red are my new little dancing shoon.

Winter Joys

White stars falling gently,
Softly down to earth,
Red fires burning brightly
In the warm and cozy hearth.
White trees changed to elfin-land,
By red sun's dazzling glow,
Little robin redbreasts
Hopping in the snow.
Happy children's voices,
Shouting loud with glee,
Oh! The joys of winter
Are wonderful to me.

Color

The world is full of color!
'Tis Autumn once again
And leaves of gold and crimson
Are lying in the lane.
There are brown and yellow acorns,
Berries and scarlet haws,

Amber gorse and heather
Purple across the moors!
Green apples in the orchard,
Flushed by a glowing sun;
Mellow pears and brambles
Where colored pheasants run!
Yellow, blue and orange,
Russet, rose and red
A gaily colored pageant
An autumn flower bed
Beauty of light and shadow,
Glory of wheat and rye,
Color of shining water
Under a sunset sky!

Rainbow Bridge

There's a bridge of wondrous light
Filled with colors shining bright
Red and orange, yellow, green,
The fairest colors ever seen,
Blue and violet, magic rose;
Down from heaven to earth it goes

Quiet Time

Now I take the brush so gently
In my hand with loving care
Watch the color flow so softly

On the paper clean and clear.

Over the Rainbow Bridge

Here we go, to and fro,
over the rainbow bridge we go.
Treading softly, treading slow,
over the rainbow bridge we go.
Gathering light from sun and star,
gathering light from heaven afar,
Down to earth all things to greet,
sharing the light with all we meet.
Here we go, to and fro,
over the rainbow bridge we go.
Treading softly, treading slow,
over the rainbow bridge we go.

Springtime Egg

By the bushes on the green,
A little bunny can be seen,
With shiny paints – red, yellow, blue,
To paint a springtime egg for you!

Golden Butterfly

Come golden butterfly, close to me,
Your beautiful golden wings,
I should like to see.

You fly like a bird,
you sip like a bee,
But you're really a flower
the wind has set free.

Little Fairy Folk

Two little clouds one summer's day
Went flying through the sky.
They went so fast they bumped their heads,
And both began to cry.

Old Father Sun looked out and said,
Oh, never mind my dears,
I'll send my little fairy folk
To dry your falling tears.

One fairy came in violet,
And one in indigo,
In blue, green, yellow, orange, red,
They made a pretty row.

They wiped the clouds tears all away,
And then out from the sky,
Upon a line the sunbeams made,
They hung their gowns to dry.

Flower Family

Radiant Sun
from his throne in the sky
Looked down on earth
where sleeping seeds lie
And thought to himself,
"I think it's time
For flower babies to
wake up and play."
So with his rays of gold
he knocked and knocked
At each and every flower family's door,
"Wake up! Wake up!" he chuckled with glee,
"Time to wake up and color the earth's floor!"
The snowdrops were first,
then crocus and rosies,
Daffodils, violets and all sorts of posies
Yawning and stretching under radiant sun,
Yes, all flowers create springtime fun!

Rainbow Dreams

In dreams of the rainbow, colors unfold,
Vibrant and magical, stories untold.
With brush in hand, let your heart take flight,
Paint the colors of the rainbow, shining bright.

Golden Sunset

As the sun sets in a golden haze,
The sky ablaze with its fiery rays.
Brush strokes of gold and hues of red,
Capture the beauty before the day is shed.

Whispering Woods

In the depths of the whispering woods,
Where secrets are shared among trees' hoods,
Let greens and browns dance on the canvas,
As nature's harmonies unfold with grace.

Starry Night

Beneath a sky of twinkling stars,
Where the moon casts its radiant bars,
Let your brush capture the midnight glow,
Painting a masterpiece, as dreams bestow.

Autumn's Tapestry

As leaves fall in a symphony of hues,
Crimson, amber, and golden views.
Embrace the colors of autumn's embrace,
And create a tapestry with nature's grace.

Whimsical Waves

In a land where the ocean meets the sky,
Whimsical waves dance as seagulls fly.
Paint the azure waters with strokes of blue,
And let the colors merge in a seaside view.

Enchanted Forest

In the heart of an enchanted forest glade,
Where fairies dance and
woodland creatures wade.
With emerald greens and
hints of dappled light,
Capture the mystical essence
in your painting's sight.

Painting Through the Seasons

The use of colors in painting allows us to create a rich tapestry of moods, reflecting the seasons and the festivals of the year, guiding the child towards a deeper understanding of the natural world. These suggestions can be adapted to different regions and their unique climates and celebrations, fostering a sense of connection to the environment and the cycles of life.

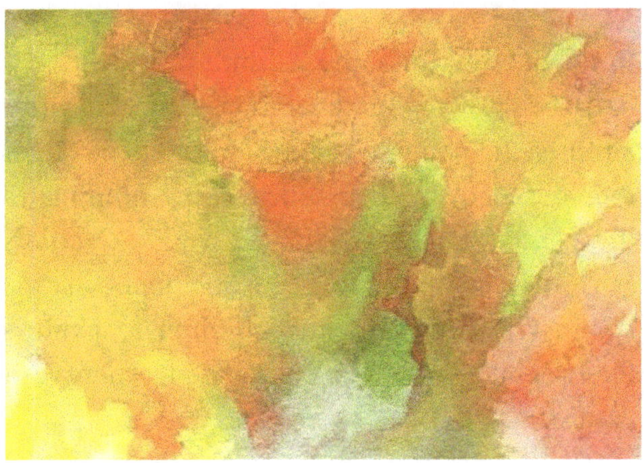

In the winter season, the ethereal blues hold great significance. Through the varying tones of light to dark, children can create enchanting winter pictures on the white canvas, evoking a sense of wonder and awe in their hearts.

As spring emerges, delicate shades of lemon yellow to ultramarine blue bring joy to the children's painting experiences. The meeting of blue and yellow gives birth to a gentle light green, unraveling the mystery of nature's verdant beauty. This interplay of light and darkness in the colors offers a glimpse into the transformative forces of growth and renewal. The vibrant hues of golden yellow and vermillion capture the spirit of Easter, as children dab red, yellow, and blue spots on a green background, filling their artwork with a joyful Easter atmosphere.

In the summertime, the warmth of radiant red, luminous yellow, and vibrant orange inspires children to paint with passion. Red becomes the courageous hero, while yellow illuminates the world with its radiant glow. These colors mirror the vitality and exuberance of the summer season, allowing children to express their connection to the abundant energy of nature.

During the autumn season, a magical atmosphere fills the air, reaching its peak on Halloween when we have the opportunity to work wonders with colors. But how do we unlock this enchantment? We invite the children to embark on a colorful journey, allowing them to create various patches of red, blue, and yellow on their canvas. Red, the mighty magician, holds the power to transform these patches, revealing their hidden potential. With utmost care and precision, the children diligently paint over the blue patches, watching them turn into shades of violet and mauve. They then turn their attention to the yellow patches, magically transforming them into vibrant shades of orange. This process captivates the school children, each bringing their unique temperament to the task, immersing themselves in the activity with varying levels of concentration.

We can also paint:

Today Red, the magician, is going around,
Very soon the Yellow he's found
And made him orange without a sound.

Or at Halloween itself:

On Halloween night if only
you knew Quick Red,
He played a trick on old Blue.
Old Blue turned red, and Red turned blue,
And no one could tell me who was who.

But that all happened in the best of fun
And now they're both purple all in one.

As November arrives and nature presents us with muted hues of browns and grays, a subtle transformation takes place within us. The colors, like dormant embers, begin to ignite, radiating warmth and light from within. The children sense this inner illumination, and with quiet determination, they seek to create something particularly beautiful for their beloved parents.

In their artistic endeavors, they gravitate towards the soothing tones of blue and violet, reflecting the serene and contemplative mood of the season. With each brushstroke, they infuse their paintings with love and gratitude, expressing their heartfelt appreciation for the nurturing presence of their father and mother.

In this way, the children connect with the rich tapestry of autumn's colors, not only on a visual level but also on a soulful and spiritual level. They learn to discern the subtle nuances of shades and tones, understanding how colors can evoke specific moods and emotions.

It's always good to set the Advent mood with Christmas at the door:

See in that blue
As dark as night
A star breaks through
Of yellow bright.

Through their creative exploration, they cultivate a deep appreciation for the interplay of colors and their transformative potential. Painting becomes a medium through which they can express their inner world, sharing their unique perspectives and experiences with others. In this harmonious blend of artistry and reverence, the children find joy and fulfillment, their paintings serving as a testament to the beauty that lies within themselves and the world around them.

Through this process, they develop a deeper appreciation for the ever-changing beauty of the natural world. By engaging with colors in their paintings, children cultivate a profound connection to the rhythms of nature and the seasonal cycles.

Through their artistic expressions, they gain insight into the interplay of light and darkness, the transformation of colors, and the harmony that exists in the natural world. The act of painting becomes a pathway for them to explore and celebrate the wonders of creation, fostering a sense of reverence and wonder for the world around them.

Why Color Stories and Verses

Engaging in the vibrant world of painting with colors, we witness a profound relationship unfolding between the child and the hues that dance upon the canvas.

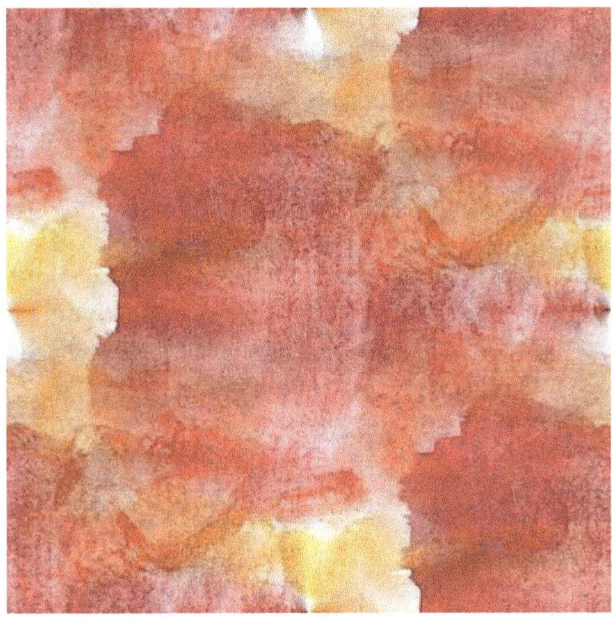

As we embark on this artistic journey, we discover that it is not merely about the finished picture but the rich experience that accompanies it. Through the interplay of colors, a tapestry of stories and rhymes emerges, enveloping the child in a captivating realm where imagination and expression intertwine.

In this enchanting process, the child forges a deep connection with the colors, as if they possess a life of their own. Conversing and playing with the vibrant hues, the child becomes one with the painting, immersed in a world where each stroke carries a meaningful conversation. The colors become companions, guiding the child's artistic exploration, and igniting the spark of creativity.

The resulting artwork is not merely a static representation but a testament to the dynamic exchange between the child and the colors. With joy and anticipation, the child shares their creation, unveiling delightful surprises hidden within the vibrant hues. These stories and rhymes interweave with the memory of the experience, fostering mental agility and nurturing the development of nuanced concepts and emotions.

While some children readily dive into the painting process, others may need time to fully embrace the dance of colors. Patience and gentle guidance become essential, offering hints and reciting rhymes that kindle the child's curiosity and deepen their connection with the hues. Each child requires their own pace, and it is vital to honor their unique rhythm, allowing them to fully engage and unfold their artistic expression.

When painting together in a group, it is crucial to create an environment that respects each child's individual journey. Transitioning out of the activity should be done gradually, providing space for the child's connection with the colors to find a natural conclusion. Abrupt interruptions can disrupt the flow and hinder the child's immersion in the painting process.

Through this mindful and nurturing approach to painting with colors, we cultivate an environment where the child's imagination flourishes. They develop a reverence for the beauty and transformative power of colors, fostering mental flexibility and nurturing the unfolding of multifaceted thoughts and emotions. Within this colorful tapestry of stories and artistry, the child's creative journey becomes a vessel for self-expression, growth, and the exploration of the wondrous world of imagination.

Experiencing the Colors

In painting, children embark on a profound journey of discovery as they encounter the unique characteristics and interactions of colors. Through the act of painting, colors come alive, engaging in vibrant conversations and playful dances. When children explore the realm of colors, the dynamics shift depending on whether they work with two colors or introduce a broader palette.

While young children aged two or three may find joy in painting with a single color, older children seek a more expansive experience. The limitations of a solitary hue soon exhaust its expressive capacity, prompting children to immerse themselves in a colorful symphony that fills the canvas.

However, there are certain colors that hold distinct qualities even when painted in isolation. Blue, for instance, unveils a world of possibilities when used on its own. Through variations of light and dark blue, contours emerge, giving rise to majestic mountains, rolling waves, rugged cliffs, and mysterious caves. Older children often yearn for defined forms, and blue fulfills their desire with its ability to manifest clear boundaries.

Painting solely with red can evoke a spirited energy within children, sometimes even igniting a wildness in their artistic expression. Yet, a picture composed entirely of red tends to lack visual harmony and beauty.

Yellow presents a unique challenge when used as the sole color, as it possesses an inherent inclination to cascade off the paper. Its radiant nature seeks companionship, requiring the presence of a second color to anchor its vibrant streams.

Violet, orange, and green are not mere combinations of red and blue, red and yellow, or blue and yellow, but rather distinct colors with individual characteristics. In the natural world, green reveals its multifaceted nature, conveying solemnity and even a hint of oppression in the mighty pine trees and holly bushes, while offering a soothing and relaxing presence in the gentle meadows. Mauve violet tones exude a solemn festivity or occasionally an air of pomp, while orange radiates cheerfulness or, at times, a hint of aggression.

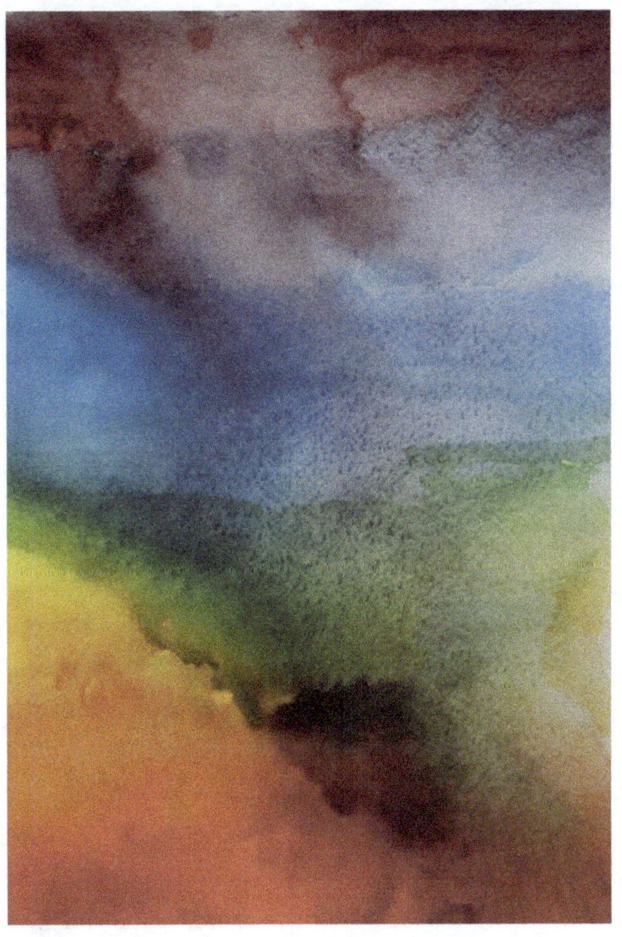

It is essential for older children to experience violet, orange, and green as independent colors. To truly grasp their unique qualities, these hues should be used straight from the tube, with water added to activate their inherent essence. Mixing two component colors in a single pot does not capture the true nature of these shades. The magic unfolds when the colors blend on the canvas during the painting process. When red and blue intertwine, vibrant violet emerges. When red joins forces with yellow, playful orange bursts forth. And when blue encounters yellow, the serene and verdant green takes shape.

Rudolf Steiner gives an example of how to bring color experience to school children:

"But let us awaken in the child what it means to look at black, red, green, yellow, white. Let us call up in him what it is when we surround a point by a circle. Let us call up the great experience contained in the difference there is when we draw two green circles and in each of them three red circles, then two red and in each of them three green, two yellow with three blue ones in them, then two blue containing three yellow circles. We let the children experience in the colors what the colors as such are saying to the human being, for in the world of color lives a whole world. But we also let the children experience what the colors have to say to one another, what green says to red, what blue says to yellow, blue to green and red to blue - here we have

the most wonderful relation between the colors."

This approach stands in contrast to the simplified mixtures children often learn about. The traditional notion that yellow and red create orange, blue and yellow yield green, and red and blue form violet fails to capture the depth and richness of the colors' true interactions. Through the act of painting, children immerse themselves in a world where colors hold the power to surprise, delight, and inspire, revealing their enchanting secrets as they come alive on the canvas.

Moods of Nature

The captivating moods found in nature's embrace, whether within the depths of the forest, along the tranquil waters, amidst the vibrant meadows, or within the contrasting moments of morning and evening, thunderstorms, storms, and scorching summer days, serve as inspiration for older children (aged 9 to 13) to explore the realm of painting. However, it is crucial that the chosen motif arises from the very essence of colors themselves.

In the radiance of the morning, children may select bright and vigorous hues such as golden yellow and vermilion, reflecting the vibrant energy of the early hours. Conversely, as evening casts its enchanting spell, the palette shifts to include ultramarine blue, cobalt blue, and carmine red, evoking a sense of tranquility and depth. Throughout the painting process, the interplay of colors gives rise to the emergence of orange and violet, enhancing the richness of the composition.

The exploration of a thunderstorm led to a unique experience as black joined the array of colors. Witnessing the children's fascination with the various shades of gray that manifested during their encounter with black was truly remarkable.

During a dedicated painting lesson, the journey unfolded gradually, allowing each child to express their individuality based on their age, temperament, and inherent nature. Guided by the presence of cobalt blue, ultramarine blue, dark yellow, and vermilion, the children initially painted with a sense of freedom, immersing themselves in the exploration of these color harmonies. On a second sheet, they delved deeper into the intricate interplay of these hues, delving into the nuances of their relationships.

Finally, on a third sheet, they unleashed their creative spirit, giving form and life to their own unique expressions. Through this process, vibrant pictures reminiscent of a blossoming summer emerged, capturing the essence and spirit of the season.

Through the medium of painting, children embark on a transformative journey, where colors become their companions and guides.

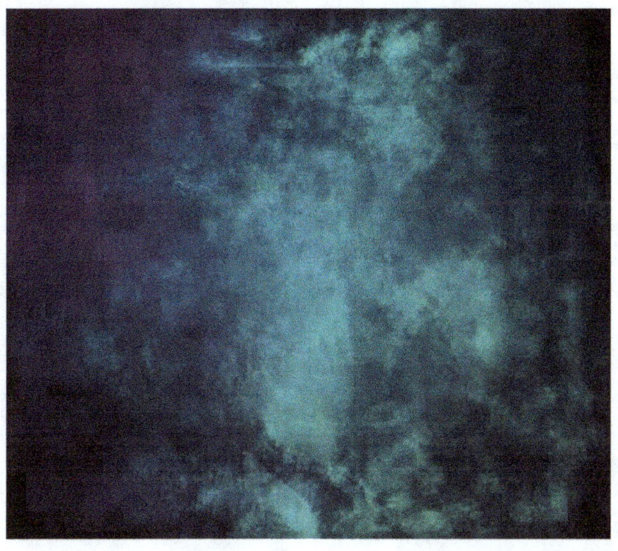

They unlock the beauty and intricacies of nature's ever-changing moods, infusing their artwork with the very essence of their experiences. With every brushstroke, guided by the interplay of vibrant hues, a world of wonder and harmony unfolds, reflecting the intricate tapestry of the natural world that surrounds them.

Painting What You See

When children engage in watercolor painting, their creative instincts are awakened, and they are eager to depict the world around them - the trees, houses, streets, and all the elements of their surroundings. The fluidity of the watercolor allows their imagination to take flight, as they bring their imagined visions to life on the paper.

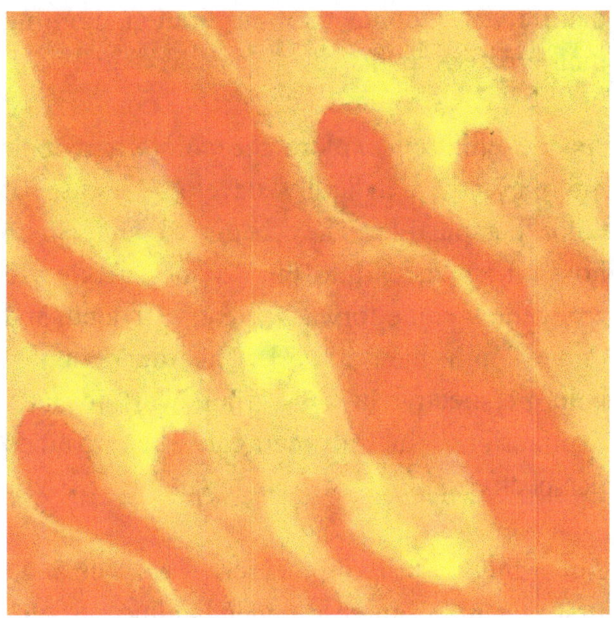

In this process, the children feel liberated from the constraints of precise contours, exact forms, and predetermined colors. Instead, they are guided by the colors themselves, which evoke certain moods and emotions, leading them to discover the essence of their artistic expression.

For children who may not resonate with other artistic mediums, painting with the brush and watercolors becomes a means for them to authentically express themselves. The colors themselves become their inspiration, igniting their creative spark.

As the children explore the colors and their interplay, they naturally develop a sense of color perspective. They begin to understand how blue recedes into the distance, while red and yellow come forward, creating a depth and dimension in their artwork. This foundation of color perspective lays the groundwork for later explorations in geometrically constructed perspectives.

According to Rudolf Steiner, it is crucial to first nurture an intense understanding of color perspective before introducing older children to traditional linear perspective. This approach ensures a holistic development of their artistic abilities and fosters a deep appreciation for the inherent beauty and harmony of colors.

Painting With Plant Pigments

Through the use of plant pigments, children are given a unique opportunity to connect with the colorful essence of the world. Just as colors in nature blend and intermingle, whether in the vast expanse of the sky or within a delicate dewdrop, they also come alive when we paint with plant-based colors.

From the very preparation of the colors, the children are captivated by the magical transformation taking place before their eyes. As they begin to paint, they are surprised to discover that the colors on the paper are not as vibrant as they appeared in the pots. Yet, this subtlety and softness remains even after multiple layers of paint have been applied. Delicate nuances and graceful transitions emerge as one color is gently laid over another, creating new tones and shades.

This experience instills a sense of wonder in the children, as they realize the special qualities inherent in these plant colors. They develop a deep affection for painting with these hues, recognizing their delicate purity and unique characteristics.

In the process, it seems as though the children are touched by the enchantment of the living elemental world, as if the very essence of nature's magic permeates their creations. Painting with plant colors becomes a profound and meaningful connection to the vibrant tapestry of life.

To prepare for painting with plant colors, a different process is followed compared to watercolors. The first step is to pound a small amount of color powder, approximately a knife point full, along with around 30 drops of resin emulsion in a mortar using a pestle. Allow the mixture to stand for a few minutes, or alternatively, grind the color powder first and then add the emulsion.

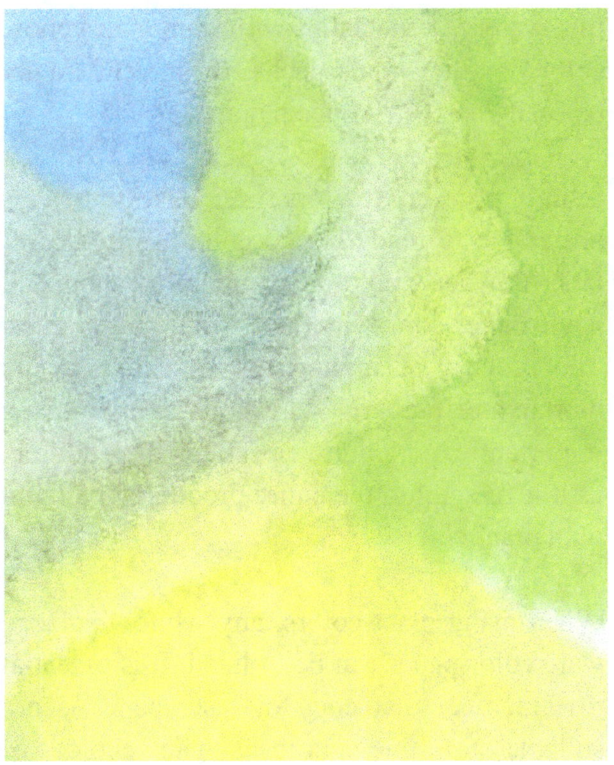

Next, add water drop by drop to the mixture using a clean paintbrush or dropper, continuously stirring until the water, powder, and emulsion are thoroughly combined. The duration of mixing may vary for each color.

Once the solution has been mixed, it can be further diluted in a jar by slowly adding water from a jug. Take care not to make the solution too watery, especially with red and yellow colors, as the small specks of pigment cannot be easily corrected once painted.

Using powdery colors in glass tubes is preferable to ready-mixed colors in bottles or jars. Powdery colors are more economical, have better longevity, and offer purer hues. The process of mixing the materials in the mortar and preparing the colors becomes an important experiential aspect for the children, as it is integral to the entire process of painting with plant colors.

When using plant colors, any white, unglazed watercolor paper can be utilized. It is essential to remember that copy or laser paper is not suitable for this purpose. The choice of appropriate paper ensures optimal absorption and interaction with the plant colors during the painting process.

Summary of Directions:

- Pound the color powder (about a knife point full) and the resin emulsion (approximately 30 drops) in a mortar with a pestle.
- Allow the mixture to stand for a few minutes or grind the color powder first and then add the emulsion.
- Add water drop by drop to the mixture, stirring continuously until the water, powder, and emulsion are evenly distributed.
- Dilute the solution further in a jar by slowly adding water from a jug, being careful not to make it too watery.
- Use powdery colors in glass tubes for better economy, longevity, and purity.
- Mixing the materials in the mortar and preparing the colors are important experiences for the children.
- Use white, unglazed watercolor paper for painting with plant pigments.
- Avoid using copy or laser paper as it is not suitable for this purpose.

Setting the Mood

To create a meaningful and engaging painting experience, it is important to set the right mood and engage the children's imagination. Start the lesson by incorporating songs, poetry, or a playful game that sparks their contemplative thinking. This allows them to enter a creative mindset and be fully present for the painting activity.

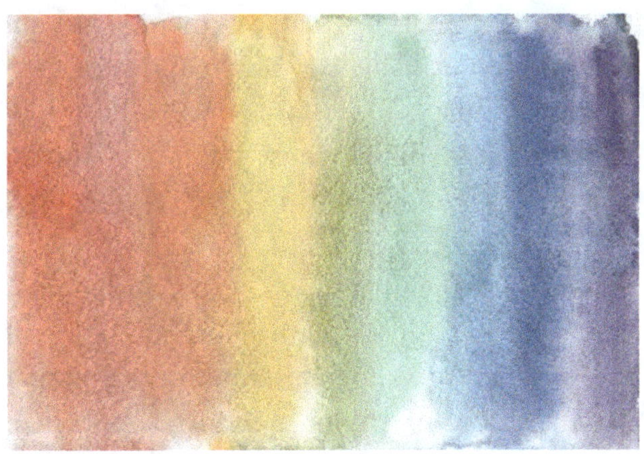

As the teacher, take the lead by painting in front of the children, demonstrating the process step by step. Emphasize the importance of not focusing on drawing specific forms but instead encourage them to explore the interplay of colors. Explain how colors have their own language and can "speak" to one another when they are placed next to each other and mixed together. This approach helps the children understand the magic of color blending and the limitless possibilities it offers.

A particular favorite among the children is the creation of rainbows. Show them how with just the three primary colors, they can produce a stunning and vibrant spectrum. Rainbows hold a special fascination for children, and they often request to see them in your demonstrations. This not only captivates their attention but also reinforces the concept of color mixing and opens doors to further exploration.

As the lessons progress, introduce color studies that align with the current topics of study. This allows the children to deepen their understanding of colors within the context of other subjects. Provide them with the freedom to choose whether they want to replicate what you have painted or explore their own unique ideas. This cultivates their individuality and encourages their artistic expression.

In addition to guided lessons, it is important to occasionally allow the children to paint quietly on their own. This gives them the opportunity to connect with their inner artistic voice and explore their own creative visions. You will be pleasantly surprised by the sensitivity and quality of their artwork as they grow in confidence and skill.

As you observe their efforts and witness their artistic growth, you will be filled with joy and satisfaction. The children's enthusiasm and dedication to their paintings will be evident, and their unique perspectives will shine through in their artwork. The transformative power of painting in their lives will be evident as they develop a deeper connection with colors and express themselves artistically.

A Song for Painting Day

Here we go, to and fro,
over the rainbow bridge we go.
Treading softly, treading slow,
over the rainbow bridge we go;
Gathering light from sun and star,
gathering light from heaven afar,
Down to earth all things to greet,
sharing the light with all we meet.

Here we go, to and fro,
over the rainbow bridge we go.
Treading softly, treading slow
over the rainbow bridge we go.

A Painting Rhyme

There's a bridge of wondrous light
Filled with colors shining bright:
Red and orange, yellow, green,
The fairest colors ever seen,
Blue and violet, magic rose:
Down from heaven to earth it goes.

A Painting Story

Two little clouds one summer's day
Went flying through the sky.
They went so fast they bumped their heads,
And both began to cry.
Old Father Sun looked out and said,
Oh, never mind, my dears,
I'll send my little fairy folk
To dry your falling tears.
One fairy came in violet,
And one in indigo,
In blue, green, yellow, orange, red,
They made a pretty row.
They wiped the clouds tears all away,

And then from out the sky,
Upon a line the sunbeams made,
They hung their gowns to dry.

Lazure Painting

If one has ever entered the sacred space of the Goetheanum in Switzerland or a Waldorf school classroom, their eyes may have been drawn to the captivating beauty adorning the walls.

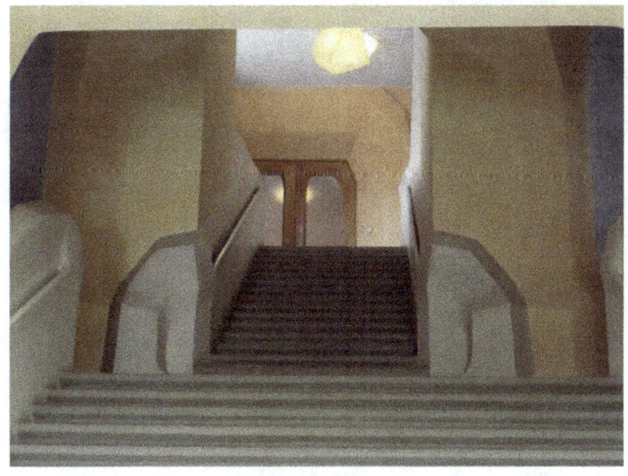

Goetheanum

Lazure painting, a remarkable decorative technique, graces these walls with its enchanting presence. Through layers of color wash delicately applied over white surfaces, Lazure allows light to pass through and reflect back, offering a pure and radiant color experience that can have a profound healing influence.

The origins of Lazure painting can be traced back to the visionary mind of Rudolf Steiner, the founder of Anthroposophy. Initially employed in the performance hall ceilings of the Goetheanum, the international headquarters of the Anthroposophical Society in Dornach, Switzerland, Lazure was conceived as a means to evoke the most luminous qualities of color. Recognizing its potential, Steiner later instructed Waldorf school teachers and parents on the application of Lazure to imbue the school walls with a living soul.

What sets Lazure apart from other decorative techniques is its reliance on the atmospheric blushing of analogous colors, rather than visual texture created by ragging or bagging. This unique approach creates a sense of movement and harmony, with colors shifting and evolving in tone throughout the day. The result is a visual symphony that soothes or enlivens the space, creating an atmosphere conducive to learning, inspiration, and inner transformation.

The colors selected for Lazure painting, carefully chosen for their pedagogical appropriateness to child development, have become the foundational palette for this remarkable decorative finish. Each color carries its own unique significance, working in harmony to create an environment that supports the growth, well-being, and creative expression of children.

Beyond the walls of Waldorf schools, Lazure painting has found its way into various spaces around the world. Its captivating allure has breathed life into homes, offices, places of worship, restaurants, and even medical and therapeutic institutions. By enveloping these spaces with the transformative power of color, Lazure painting enhances the human experience, inviting a deeper connection to the environment and nurturing the human spirit.

As we marvel at the ethereal beauty of Lazure-adorned walls, let us acknowledge the profound legacy of Rudolf Steiner and his visionary contributions to the realms of art, education, and human consciousness. Through the luminous brushstrokes of Lazure painting, we are reminded of the transformative potential of color and the enduring impact it can have on our lives.

In gratitude for the artistry of color and the wisdom of Rudolf Steiner, we celebrate the radiant beauty of Lazure painting and its transformative influence on our shared spaces. May the enchanting hues of Lazure continue to grace our surroundings, uplifting our spirits and nurturing our souls, as we journey towards a harmonious and vibrant world.

Lazure Painting Figure 8's

In the practice of Lazure painting, the lemniscate or figure 8 pattern holds profound significance and serves a specific purpose. Derived from the shape of the infinity symbol (∞) or the lemniscate, this pattern represents the eternal cycle of life and the interconnectedness of all things. By incorporating the lemniscate pattern into the painting technique, it aims to create a harmonious and balanced flow of colors throughout the space.

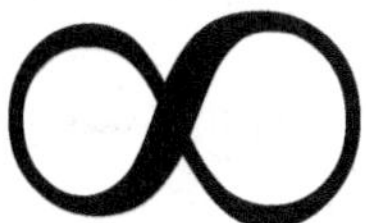

The lemniscate pattern symbolizes the continuous movement and interplay of energies within Lazure painting. As the brush moves in a figure 8 motion, it reflects the dynamic interaction between light and color, infusing the painted surface with a sense of rhythm and vitality. This rhythmic flow enhances the overall aesthetic and creates a profound sense of harmony and unity within the space.

Moreover, the lemniscate pattern aligns with the principles of anthroposophy, the philosophical and spiritual foundation of Waldorf education. In anthroposophy, the lemniscate is regarded as a symbol of wholeness and equilibrium, encompassing the interconnectedness of the physical, emotional, and spiritual dimensions of human existence. By incorporating this pattern in Lazure painting, it seeks to evoke a sense of holistic well-being and create an environment that nurtures the senses and fosters a harmonious atmosphere.

Beyond its aesthetic appeal, the lemniscate or figure 8 pattern in Lazure painting embodies profound symbolism. It invites us to contemplate the interconnectedness of all things, reminding us of the eternal cycle of life and the inherent unity of existence. Through the rhythmic flow of colors, it invites us to immerse ourselves in the beauty and harmony of the painted space, connecting us to a deeper sense of wholeness and unity.

The enchanting art of Lazure painting brings an atmosphere of wonder and beauty to spaces where it is employed. The gentle interplay of colors and the luminosity they exude create a transformative experience for those who encounter them. Whether in a Waldorf school, a home, or other settings, Lazure painting enlivens and uplifts the human spirit, inviting a deeper connection with the surrounding environment.

Lazure Painting Step-by-Step

Below is a step-by-step guide for beginners on Lazure painting, designed to assist you in bringing your envisioned magical space to life.

Materials:

- Clear acrylic glaze (Benjamin Moore Aura eggshell or any artist-grade acrylic)
- Pigment brushes (2 large soft bristled brushes)
- Soft pool cleaning brushes (2 larger and softer brushes)
- Rags for streaks and drying brushes
- Drop cloths
- Assortment of containers (2.5 quarts, plastic shoebox, 5-gallon, 2-gallon, multi-opening)
- Step ladders

Step 1: Prepare the Glaze Mixture

- Mix the clear glaze medium with water in a 1:5 ratio (1 pint glaze to 5 pints water).

- Stir the mixture thoroughly to prevent settling.
- Pour a portion of the glaze into a shoebox container.

Step 2: Apply the Clear Glaze Base

- Using a pigment brush, work the watery glaze onto the brush in a circular motion.
- Start at the center of a wall, either at the ceiling or a corner.
- Apply the clear glaze gently and quickly in a figure 8 pattern, back and forth.
- Watch out for drips that may form a minute after application, especially where you started with a freshly dipped brush.
- Smooth out any drips with the brush.
- Complete one wall, then move to the next, starting at the top and moving over and down.
- Continue to the opposite wall and finish with the back wall.
- The clear coat will serve as the base for the subsequent tinted layers.

Step 3: Mix the Tint Glazes

- Choose your desired colors for tinting.
- Mix a 2" squeeze of tube paint or 2 tablespoons of concentrated tint from a kit with a small amount of the 1:5 clear glaze mixture.
- Stir until well mixed.
- Add a quart of the 1:5 glaze and stir again.
- Add 1 quart of water to achieve a 1:10 glaze ratio.
- Optionally, add a small amount of latex paint extender to slow down drying.
- The consistency of the glaze should be waterier than watercolor.

Step 4: Apply the Tinted Layers

- Pour the two starting colors into either side of a two-sided bucket.
- Dip the brush used for the clear coat, starting with the lightest color.
- Begin adding color to the wall from the same center or corner where the clear glaze started.
- Always start with light colors and gradually work your way to darker shades.

- Blend each new patch of paint into the wet border to create a seamless transition.
- Use a gentle dry brushing technique to blend the colors while keeping the paint edge wet.
- Have one person apply the wet glaze while others dry brush behind to blend the colors.
- Ensure that the border remains wet at all times and avoid blending or painting onto a dry surface.

Step 5: Dry and Assess

- Allow the painted walls to dry completely.
- Check for any streaks and gently dry brush them out.
- Take a break and let the paint fully dry before proceeding.

Step 6: Apply the Second Coat

- For the second coat, you can add more tint to the glaze mixture if desired.
- Apply the second layer following the same process as the first coat.

- Start at the top and move down, blending lighter colors into darker shades.
- Dry brush the paint until no streaks are visible and the colors are well blended.

Step 7: Add Accent Colors and Seal

- Once the second layer has dried completely, add accent colors to specific areas if desired.
- Blend the accent colors into the previous layer using a wet clear coat border.
- Dry brush and blend the accent colors as needed.
- Once the walls are completely dry, seal the painted surface with a clear coat of your 1:5 glaze mixture.
- Apply the clear coat evenly, ensuring full coverage.

Step 8: Final Assessment and Finishing Touches

- Take a step back and assess the overall appearance of the painted walls.

- Make any necessary touch-ups or adjustments to ensure a seamless and harmonious finish.
- Stand back and admire the transformative effect of the Lazure painting technique.

Congratulations! You have successfully completed your Lazure painting project, creating a mesmerizing interplay of translucent colors in your space. Enjoy the ever-shifting tones and the enchanting atmosphere it brings to your environment.

Conclusion

In concluding this book, we reflect upon the profound journey we have undertaken through the world of colors and art, guided by the principles of anthroposophy and Waldorf education. We have explored the significance of color as a means of self-expression and its transformative power in the lives of children.

Throughout this book, we have delved into the role of art in nurturing the holistic development of the child. We have recognized the importance of providing children with opportunities to engage with colors, fostering their imagination, creativity, and inner growth. By immersing themselves in the vibrant realm of colors, children can experience a profound connection with the world around them.

We have also examined the moral and ethical aspects of color, recognizing its potential to evoke certain qualities and states of being. The exploration of Goethe's Wheel of Color has deepened our understanding of the interplay between light and darkness, warmth and coolness, and the harmonious relationships within the color spectrum.

With practical guidance and step-by-step instructions, we have embarked on a journey of painting, from preparing to paint with watercolors to exploring the use of plant pigments. We have witnessed the enchantment and wonder that arise when colors come alive on the canvas, and the significance of color stories and verses in creating a rich and meaningful painting experience.

We have embraced the seasons and the moods of nature, allowing their influences to shape our artistic endeavors. From capturing the vibrant hues of spring to expressing the tranquility of autumn, we have celebrated the ever-changing palette of the natural world.

In our exploration, we have discovered the transformative power of painting what we see, transcending the limitations of form and embracing the interplay of colors as they dance on the paper. And through the use of plant pigments, we have encountered a deeper connection to the living elemental world, touching the very essence of nature's magic.

Throughout this journey, we have emphasized the importance of setting the mood, creating a contemplative and participatory atmosphere for artistic expression. We have witnessed the beauty and sensitivity that emerge when children are given the space and freedom to explore colors and their infinite possibilities.

As we bring this book to a close, we express our gratitude to all those who have contributed to its creation. Our journey into the realm of colors has been enriched by the wisdom and insights of many individuals, and we extend our heartfelt appreciation for their inspiration and guidance.

May this book continue to inspire educators, parents, and all those passionate about nurturing the artistic spirit of children. May it serve as a guide, inviting us to embark on our own colorful explorations, unlocking the transformative power of art in the lives of children and fostering a deeper connection to the world of colors and beauty.

With reverence for the artistry of the human soul and the enchantment of colors, we conclude this book, knowing that it will continue to illuminate and inspire for years to come.

Blessings on your artistic journey!

Recommended Reading

Colour.
By Rudolf Steiner
Publisher: Rudolf Steiner Press; 2nd edition
Paperback: 224 pages
ISBN-13: 978-1855840850

Colour Dynamics: Workbook for Water Colour Painting and Colour Theory.
By Angela Lord
Publisher: Hawthorn Press
Paperback: 128 pages
ISBN-13: 978-1907359927

Drawing & Painting in Rudolf Steiner Schools.
By Fritz Weitmann and Margit Junemann
Publisher: Hawthorn Press
Paperback: 206 pages
ISBN-13: 978-1869890414

Painting and Drawing in Waldorf Schools Classes 1 to 8.
By Thomas Wildgruber
Publisher: Floris Books
Paperback: 384 pages
ISBN-13: 978-0863158780

Painting in Waldorf Education.
By Dick Bruin and Attie Lichthart
Publisher: The Association of Waldorf Schools of North America; 2nd edition
Paperback: 212 pages
ISBN-13: 978-1888365504

Painting With Children: Colour and Child Development.
By Brunhild Müller
Publisher: Floris Books; 4th edition
Paperback: 48 pages
ISBN-13: 978-0863153662

The Author

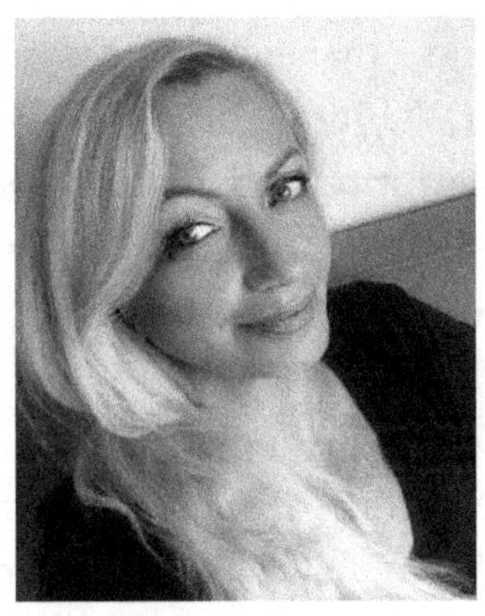

Kytka Hilmar-Jezek stands as a highly accomplished author, renowned for her influential books that have left an indelible mark on readers. With a focus on parenting, education, entrepreneurship, and natural healing, her extensive repertoire of over twenty-five thought-provoking works has earned her widespread recognition, including a place in the Revolution in Education Hall of Fame.

Kytka is a well-known figure in the Waldorf education community. Her contributions to homeschooling and Waldorf-inspired education are widely recognized. In 1996, she founded Waldorf Homeschoolers, a website that provided a wealth of resources, including over 5,000 articles and curriculum materials. (No, she no longer owns it.) Additionally, she initiated and managed the yahoo group W.I.S.H. (Waldorf Inspired Students at Home), a platform for parents and educators to connect and share ideas where at one time there were over 50,000 members.

In Bellevue, Washington, Kytka played a crucial role as one of the founding parents of Three Cedars Waldorf School. Her dedication and commitment to the Waldorf philosophy helped establish the school and create a nurturing learning environment for children.

Kytka's involvement extended beyond education as she was also the owner of Hedgehog Farms catalog. This venture showcased a selection of products aligned with the principles of Waldorf education, offering parents and educators a convenient resource for finding Waldorf-inspired materials.

With her extensive experience and involvement in the Waldorf community, Kytka brings a wealth of knowledge and expertise to this book. Her deep understanding of Waldorf education and her passion for homeschooling make her an authoritative voice in the field.

Kytka's passion for education shines through her books, which boldly challenge conventional schooling paradigms and stimulate discussions on alternative approaches. Notable titles such as "*The Smartest Kids Don't Go to School*," "*The Smartest Kids Learn All the Time*," and "*The Smartest Kids Know Their Options*" offer fresh perspectives, urging readers to question traditional norms and embrace innovative methods of nurturing children in the technological age.

Her debut book, "*Reiki for Children*," quickly soared to become a global bestseller in 2001, resonating with professionals in the field who employ it as a valuable resource in teaching children. Expanding her healing-focused publications, Hilmar-Jezek has authored works like "*Raw Food for Children*," "*Eat the Light: The Raw Food Diet as a Spiritual Practice*," "*The Ultimate Beginner's Guide to Reiki*," and "*The Rainbow Tower*," a captivating exploration of Chakras designed for young readers.

Kytka's engaging books consistently enlighten, inspire, and challenge readers on controversial and thought-provoking subjects related to health and wellness, parenting, spirituality, and education. Through her publishing houses, Distinct Press and Czech Revival Publishing, she actively promotes diverse voices across various literary genres, fostering a platform for aspiring authors to share their unique perspectives. With her remarkable versatility, she has ghostwritten over 200 books for clients worldwide and translated more than 100 books from the Czech language.

Kytka Hilmar-Jezek's journey as an accomplished author and book editor is marked by an unwavering dedication to exploring unconventional approaches to education, parenting, health, and personal growth. Her thought-provoking books, advocacy for diverse voices, and commitment to preserving cultural heritage have made a profound impact on the literary world. By delving into her works, readers embark on a transformative journey that challenges norms, inspires critical thinking, and fosters positive change in their lives and communities.

Outside her literary endeavors and now that her children are grown, Kytka finds joy in various ventures, such as her contributions to TresBohemes.com, where she has penned numerous posts on Czech culture. Her commitment to preserving cultural heritage is further evident in her work preserving old photographs for The Photo Vault and curating items for The Czech Museum. Most of all, she loves to read on lazy afternoons, snuggled next to her Shiba Inu, Richard.

Learn more at kytkajezek.com.

www.ingramcontent.com/pod-product-compliance
Lightning Source LLC
LaVergne TN
LVHW020051110826
845155LV00021B/68
* 9 7 8 1 9 4 3 1 0 3 3 4 8 *